TRAVELLERS

MOROCCO

By
JAMES KEEBLE

Written by James Keeble, updated by Claire Boobbyer
Original photography by Ian Burgum

Published by Thomas Cook Publishing
A division of Thomas Cook Tour Operations Limited.
Company registration no. 3772199 England
The Thomas Cook Business Park, Unit 9, Coningsby Road,
Peterborough PE3 8SB, United Kingdom
Email: books@thomascook.com, Tel: + 44 (0) 1733 416477
www.thomascookpublishing.com

Produced by Cambridge Publishing Management Limited
Burr Elm Court, Main Street, Caldecote CB23 7NU

ISBN: 978-1-84848-151-0

© 2005, 2007 Thomas Cook Publishing
This third edition © 2009
Text © Thomas Cook Publishing
Maps © Thomas Cook Publishing

Project Editor: Adam Royal
Series Editor: Maisie Fitzpatrick
Production/DTP: Steven Collins

Printed and bound in Italy by Printer Trento

Cover photography: Front L–R: © Carmen Sedano/Alamy; © Giocoso
Paolo/SIME/4Corners Images; © Ripani Massimo/SIME/4Corners Images
Back: © Jon Arnold Images Ltd/Alamy

Contents

KEY TO MAPS

✈	Airport
▲ *736m*	Mountain
★	Start of walk/drive
i	Information
☀	Viewpoint
—	City wall
■	POI

4

Introduction

Morocco is the oldest kingdom in the Muslim world. History is always present here, in the breathtaking architecture of imperial cities and of desert kasbahs, and in ancient tombs scattering the hillsides.

The gateway to Africa, westernmost outpost of Islam, Morocco lies a mere 14km (9 miles) across the Straits of Gibraltar from Spain. Despite its close proximity to Europe it is a land still veiled in mystery for most Westerners, an exotic kingdom that intrigues and inspires. Here are the sights and smells of Arabia, the legendary souks of Fès and Marrakech overflowing with colourful carpets and pungent spices. Yet here, too, are the rhythms and traditions of Africa, the tribal dances and camel trains of the Sahara, constant reminders of the great continent to the south.

THOMAS COOK'S MOROCCO

Morocco was first mentioned by Cook as a tourist destination in 1886, as part of a tour to Spain and Gibraltar. By the turn of the century it was being marketed as an exotic alternative for 'nomadic travel'.

The regular running of the Moroccan Express from Madrid made it more accessible, and in the 1920s and 1930s it was a popular place for motor-car tours.

This is no longer the wild land it was in the days of Barbary pirates and Saharan sheikhs. Tanger is now a rapidly expanding port. Casablanca is a modern business centre of skyscrapers and expressways. Camels have been replaced with Mercedes and motorbikes. And there is even talk of a futuristic

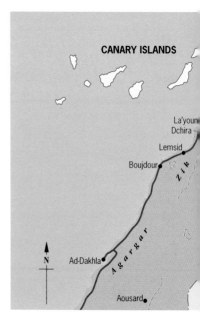

CANARY ISLANDS

La'youn
Dchira
Lemsid
Boujdour
Ad-Dakhla
Aousard

bridge or tunnel connecting Morocco and Africa with the continent of Europe. However, despite all of these developments, Morocco still surprises visitors with its subtle blend of ancient mysticism and modern-day capitalism, Arabic conservatism and African *joie de vivre*, and the country is as alluring as ever. Straddled between two seas and between two continents, Morocco is always dramatic, always unpredictable.

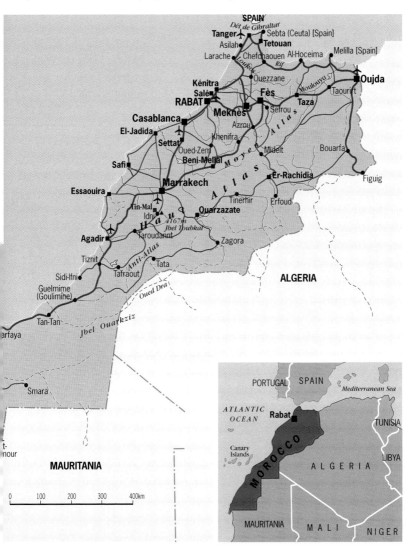

History

Prehistory *Homo erectus* has been in the Maghreb for at least 200,000 years. At this time the Sahara may have been savannah filled with wildlife.

10,000–5000 BC Neolithic era. Stone circles in the north of the country date from this era. Neolithic Moroccans were pastoralists who may have had links with northern Europeans.

1100–500 BC Trading posts are established along the coast by the Phoenicians. Settlements from Tamuda (near Tetouan) to Mogador (Essaouira) in the south bring settled agriculture and urbanisation. Carthage (Tunisia) controls much of North Africa.

146 BC–AD 250 Carthage falls to Rome. Volubilis, near Meknès, becomes capital of Roman Mauritania Tingitana. Roman influence spreads throughout Morocco.

AD 253–683 Roman withdrawal. Morocco is divided into Berber fiefdoms. Raids in North Africa by German Vandals, then Byzantines.

683–711 Arab forces invade, their leader Moussa Ibn Nasr claiming the land furthest west for Islam. His armies, bolstered by Berber converts, invade Spain in 711.

788–828 Idris I, exiled from Baghdad after the Sunni–Shiite split in Islam, is welcomed in Volubilis as ruler by local Berber tribes, establishing the first Arab dynasty – the Idrisids. He is poisoned by followers of the Caliph of Baghdad. His son Moulay Idris II develops Fès.

1062–1145 The pious Almoravid dynasty emerges from a confederation of nomadic Sanhaya Berber tribes taking advantage of bickering between Idrisid rulers. Youssef Ben Tachfine conquers as far as Spain and founds Marrakech. His ambition is to set up the ideal Islamic state, but he suppresses the arts, poetry, mysticism and intellectual curiosity that made the Idrisid dynasty great.

1147–1248 Ibn Toumert preaches a return to Islamic fundamentalism. His followers conquer territories from Spain to Libya. The Almohad dynasty is formed, ushering in a golden age of architecture, when the Hassan Tower in Rabat and the Koutoubia Minaret in Marrakech are built.

1212 Almohads are defeated by the Spanish Christians at Las Navas de Tolosa.

1248–1465 Rule of the Merenid dynasty, originating from southern desert tribes. Proliferation of arts, religious study and dazzling architecture. First to introduce the médersa. The dynasty falls when it becomes corrupt.

1465–1554 The Wattasid dynasty assumes power, led by former Merenid advisers. Centralised control wanes. Spain and Portugal establish bases. Much of rural Morocco is controlled by religious warrior factions (marabouts).

1492–1550 Spanish seize Granada, ending 700 years of Islamic rule in Andalucía. Influx of Spanish Muslim and Jewish refugees.

1554–1669 The Saadian dynasty develops from powerful southern marabouts based in the Dra Valley. Spanish and Portuguese 'infidels' are driven out. Ahmed el Mansour conquers North Africa as far as Timbuktu.

1578 Battle of the Three Kings. Young, naïve Portuguese king Sebastian is defeated at Ksar-el-Kebir.

1609 Bou Regreg pirates pillage from their base at Rabat.

1669 Emergence of the present-day Alaouite dynasty, from Rissani in the south.

1672–1727 Ruthless reign of Moulay Ismaïl, aided by an army of 150,000 slaves. Foundation of Meknès. English and Spanish are evicted from the coast. Ismaïl attempts to marry the daughter of the French king Louis XIV and to convert the English king James II to Islam.

1757–90 Reign of Sidi Mohammed.

1800–80	Civil war as Fès and Marrakech fight for dominance. Power is increasingly devolved to localised Sufi brotherhoods. Madrid Conference in 1880 establishes European control of Tanger.
1894–1908	Sultan Abd el Aziz leaves bankrupt after high spending. French troops land at Casablanca and Oujda.
1912	The Treaty of Fès grants France '*Maroc utile*' ('useful Morocco'), while Spain receives territory on the northern coast and in the deep south. Rabat becomes Morocco's new capital. Tanger is declared an international demilitarised zone.
1912–56	Tanger enjoys an international jet-set reputation. Population increases and the country's infrastructure is developed.
1942	British and American forces land at Casablanca to free Morocco.
1944	Formation of nationalist Istiqlal Party.

	Demonstrations are held demanding independence.
1953	Royal family is exiled.
1956–7	Independence from France. Mohammed V changes his title from sultan to king.
1961	Mohammed V dies. Hassan II accedes to throne.
1963	First parliamentary elections are held.
1975	The Green March: King Hassan II leads 350,000 civilians to claim Western Sahara from Spain.
1976–88	Polisario rebel fighters seek independence for Western Sahara.
1989	Moroccan–Algerian relations are restored. Union of the Maghreb (UMA) is formed between Morocco, Algeria, Tunisia, Libya and Mauritania.
1992	Western Sahara referendum postponed by UN observers after vote-rigging.
1999	Hassan II dies and his son Mohammed VI becomes his successor.

2000	EU trade agreement. Disputes with Spain continue.
2001	UN proposes a solution for problems in Western Sahara by setting it up as an autonomous state within Morocco. The Moroccan government accepts the proposal but the Polisario Front does not.
2002	Mohammed VI marries Salma Bemani, a commoner, and breaks with tradition. Increased tension between Morocco and Spain. Driss Jettou, former Interior Minister, is appointed Prime Minister by the king.
2003	Crown Prince Moulay Hassan is born. US invasion of Iraq.
2004	New Family Law is introduced: women are entitled to equal share of assets in divorce, and age of marital consent is raised to 18.
2005–6	Trade liberalisation agreements with EU, USA, Tunisia, Egypt and Jordan. The Independence Intifada, a series of peaceful protests by Sahrawis in the occupied territories, is supported by Polisario Front.
2007	Princess Laila Khadija is born. Abbas el Fassi appointed Prime Minister after the victory of the Istiqlal Party in elections.
2008	New political party, PAM, is formed by a friend of the king, Fouad Ali el Himma.

Essaouira ramparts

Imperial to colonial

When Moulay Idris arrived in Morocco in 788 he founded a tradition of imperial rule that has been the cornerstone of Moroccan history. Morocco has been governed almost continuously since then by only seven dynasties.

The Idrisids did not last long. With the death of Idris II, theological bickering among his successors paved the way for a puritanical backlash, provided by the Almoravid dynasty, which swept to power from bases in the southern desert. Rejecting Fès, the Idrisid capital, Youssef Ben Tachfine built the city of Marrakech from which to rule his expanding empire. Following Ben Tachfine's death the kingdom fell apart once more, and into the gulf stepped Ibn Toumert, a theologian with a mission to purge Islam of impurity. From his mosque at Tin-Mal he spread a fundamentalist message with passionate preaching and the sword. His followers formed the Almohad or Unitarian sect. Toumert's successor, Abd el Moumen rode into Fès and Marrakech, effectively becoming sultan of the new Almohad dynasty.

Next came the Merenids, who, having conquered Fès in 1248, started a 200-year passion for building.

Ancient architecture reflects Morocco's turbulent history

Occupied with battles in Spain, the Merenid rulers preferred to promote stability in Morocco, allowing the kingdom to become a centre of great learning and culture. In 1492 the Christians completed the reconquest of Spain and the Portuguese captured Atlantic ports, leaving the Merenids empty-handed. Following a power struggle in Fès, a group of viziers saw a chance for a coup and for the next 90 years the Wattasids clung to tenuous power, continually threatened by European raiding parties.

In the mid-16th century, the Saadians from the southern Dra

decided it was time to rid Morocco of Christian invaders. They defeated the Portuguese in 1578 but with the death of their leader, Ahmed el Mansour in 1603, chaos reigned once more. Time was ripe for a strong leader, and in 1672 the infamous Moulay Ismaïl came to the throne, the first of the present Alaouite dynasty, ruling for 55 years (the longest reign of any Moroccan monarch). Fearsome and brutal, he laid the foundations for a modern Moroccan state; he consolidated his kingdom through force and an ambitious building programme. With Morocco well established as a North African power, the 18th and 19th centuries saw growing interest from European superpowers, which all wanted a slice of the cake. Unable to withstand such might, Morocco was forced to capitulate, leading to the 1912 Treaty of Fès, which gave France most of the country, with Spain retaining the Atlantic coast. After 1,100 years, imperial rule had become colonial rule.

Fortunately, the French governor proved as wise as any of Morocco's former sultans. Marshal Lyautey was an enlightened general who immersed himself in much of Morocco's history and traditions. Through his influence much of Morocco's heritage was preserved, and its infrastructure greatly improved. Following World War II, Sultan Mohammed V proclaimed independence, supported by the USA and Britain. After much disagreement the French pulled out in 1956 and Mohammed was declared king – the 13th ruler of the Alaouite dynasty. Morocco was an empire once more.

The Koutoubia Mosque in Marrakech was built during the reign of the third Almohad caliph

The land

Medieval Arab historians and geographers used to call Morocco 'Maghreb-al-Aksa', meaning the land furthest west. It lies between the two continents of Europe and Africa. In the north its shores are just 14km (9 miles) from Spain; to the south its borders disappear into the sands of the Sahara desert.

Vital statistics

Morocco is a large country, covering 710,850sq km (274,460sq miles) since the addition of vast stretches of Western Sahara (*see p8*). Fifteen per cent of this landmass is over 2,000m (6,500ft) in altitude, making Morocco one of the most mountainous lands in Africa. Variety is its speciality: there are two coastlines – the Mediterranean, extending for 530km (329 miles), composed of cliffs and coves, and the 2,800km (1,740-mile) Atlantic coast, one long beach backed by sand dunes. Its capital, Rabat, has only been an

The kasbah of Tanger

administrative centre since 1912. Like many African countries, Morocco has seen a population explosion since the mid-20th century – from 6 million inhabitants in 1945 to 33.3 million today, and 42 million predicted by the year 2020. About 75 per cent of this population are under the age of 25.

Landscapes

The north of Morocco seems like a continuation of Europe, with a rocky coast reminiscent of the northern Mediterranean. Further south are three waves of mountains stretching from west to east – the Middle Atlas of high plateaux, inhabited by Berber tribes; the High Atlas, which stretch for 700km (435 miles) and contain 400 peaks over 3,000m (9,800ft); and the dry Anti-Atlas, following the borders of the Sahara and marking the topographical beginning of Africa.

To the west are the wide plains of the Oum er Rbia (Mother of Green) and Oued Sebou, Morocco's two greatest rivers. These expanses of fertile land contain most of Morocco's agriculture – olive trees, corn, citrus, sugar cane and vines. East to the Algerian border is a barren steppe region, merging gradually into the Sahara.

The southern desert is mostly flat and rocky. Sand dunes exist south of the Dra Valley and east of the Ziz Valley, but otherwise the Moroccan Sahara is *hamada*, stone desert. Oases are common, and provide spectacular bursts of fertility among the rocks and sand.

Climate

Marshal Lyautey, French colonial governor of Morocco, called it 'a cold country with a hot sun'. When it comes to climate, Morocco has a bit of everything. Winter temperatures in the High Atlas plunge to –10°C (14°F), and many villages are snow-bound for up to four months. In Western Sahara it is often above 50°C (122°F) in places that have not seen rain in over ten years. Spring and autumn are the best months in the south, but rain storms can cause flash floods in dry river valleys.

Sand dunes of Diabat on the Atlantic coast

In recent years Morocco has been suffering from drought, although rains have eased the water shortage. In a country dependent on agriculture, which obtains almost 80 per cent of its electricity from hydroelectric power in the High Atlas, climatic changes can still be a matter of life and death.

Economy

The Moroccan economy, thanks to a decade of reform, has been improving. However, the recent global economic downturn has meant a decrease in exports to the EU and an increase in unemployment.

Not blessed with the vast oil reserves of its neighbours Algeria and Libya, Morocco is nonetheless the largest exporter of phosphate in the world, possessing three-quarters of the world's phosphate reserves. With a decrease in phosphate prices, tourism is rapidly becoming the country's most important industry. Yet 50 per cent of the workforce are still employed in agriculture, representing a quarter of Morocco's economic output.

From countryside to city

This disparity between city and country life is a continuing problem: rural depopulation coupled with urban migration has created vast shanty towns or *bidonvilles* in many of the big cities. Casablanca has grown from a small port of 20,000 in 1900 to between 3 and 4 million today.

Culture and festivals

The indigenous population of Morocco is Berber, a people who originated in ancient Libya. Morocco contains the largest percentage of Berbers in North Africa – 60 per cent of its inhabitants. Yet waves of immigration have left Morocco with a complicated social mix, formed by intermingling communities of Arabs, Berbers, Jews and Harratins.

Origins

During the French occupation much was made of the rivalries between Arab and Berber, but today Moroccan society prides itself on being integrated, with most people describing themselves as 'Moroccan'. Although 40 per cent of the population still do not speak Moroccan Arabic as their first language, and 1,000 Berber dialects are currently spoken in scattered village communities, nationalism is a positive force even in the remote countryside. This is a liberal country within the Arab world and differences are respected, beneath the umbrella of the state. Indeed, Moroccans claim proudly that anyone can achieve anything in Morocco; their history is marked with cases of lowly slaves becoming rich sultans.

Morocco's cultural heritage is not only Arab and Berber: the country used to have the largest Jewish population in the Arab world. At independence in 1956 there were 200,000 Jews living in Morocco, but most moved to Israel following the 1967 Arab–Israeli War.

Character

Moroccans are a proud people, as befits a race that has controlled the entire western Mediterranean and produced some of the finest architecture in the Arab world. Like all Mediterraneans they are storytellers, and friendly exaggeration is the order of the day. Getting a straight answer is a skill akin to bargaining. Moroccans enjoy a reputation as the most hospitable of Arab peoples, although the lure of tourist money in the big cities is beginning to override traditional curiosity and friendliness.

Inshallah

The most common Moroccan saying, '*inshallah*', means 'if God wills'. The Moroccan mentality is directly linked to this philosophy: ultimately Allah knows all and controls all – it is better to sit and wait for his will to happen than to do things yourself. Admittedly things are changing as Morocco seeks to enter the modern business world, but a degree of fatalistic inertia still remains, as it does in many Mediterranean lands (*mañana*, in Spain, is a similar concept).

The influence of Islam is all-pervading in Moroccan daily life. Consumption of alcohol in public places is discouraged and in many places men and women do not mix socially outside the home. Yet the younger generation is changing. You will see mothers wearing veils alongside daughters in jeans and make-up. Young couples walk hand in hand, something their parents would never have done. This is a time of great change in Morocco, a transition you will soon sense (*see p24*).

Islamic fundamentalism

Far removed from the heartland of Islam, Morocco has always sought to maintain a stable society, allowing all beliefs to be shared. While Islamic fundamentalists struggle for power in neighbouring Algeria, King Mohammed VI has attempted to combine his role as Imam, leader of the faithful, with a process of economic 'Westernisation'. So far he has succeeded, and it looks unlikely that violent fundamentalism will spill over into Morocco. Yet the spectre looms on the sidelines: in 2003, 14 suicide bombers from an Islamic terrorist organisation killed 33 people in Casablanca, and two further, less damaging attacks took place there in 2007. Those found responsible for the Madrid bombings in 2004 were from the poorer areas of Salé. Extremism has taken a foothold in the areas where migrants from rural areas have congregated on the outskirts of Moroccan cities.

Most Moroccans, however, seem content with the secular and religious leadership of their country.

Street musician in Marrakech playing the *gimbri*

FESTIVALS

Moroccan festivals (*moussem*) are generally religious in inspiration. Annual pilgrimages are made to the tombs of local saints, accompanied by music and dancing. Celebrations may last for several days, when quiet country towns are transformed into encampments of tents, with itinerant food stalls, entertainers and herds of horses. Local harvests are celebrated similarly.

Several Moroccan festivals have an international reputation. These include the summer arts festival in Asilah; the June folk festival in Marrakech, in which performers from every region of Morocco descend on the ruined El Badi Palace – it's worth planning an entire trip around it; also in June, the Fès World Sacred Music Festival; and the autumn fantasia in Meknès – the most impressive in the country. The dates of many festivals vary each year, in accordance with the Muslim calendar. Contact local tourist offices for information.

At any religious festival discretion is required when taking photographs.

Principal festivals

February Almond blossom festival, Tafraoute.

March Theatre festival, Casablanca; cotton festival, Beni-Mellal.

May Rose festival, El-Kelaa-M'Gouna.

June Folk festival in the El Badi Palace, Marrakech; cherry festival, Sefrou; World Sacred Music Festival, Fès; *moussem* at Asni near Marrakech; Saharan *moussem* at Tan-Tan; camel festival, Asrir, near Guelmime.

July Honey festival, Imouzzer-Ida-Outanan; water festival, Martil near Tetouan.

August International Arts Festival, Asilah; *moussem* of Setti-Fatma, Ourika

A mock horse-back battle at Fantasia in Meknès

near Marrakech; *moussem* of Sidi Allal al Hadh, Chefchaouen; *moussem* of Moulay Abdessalem, including fantasia, near El-Jadida; festival of African music, Tiznit; apple festival, Imouzzer-Kandar.

September Fantasia in Meknès, one of the biggest festivals in Morocco; traditional arts festival, Fès; *moussem* of Moulay Idris II, when Fassi craftsmen sacrifice cattle in honour of the city's patron saint; *moussem* of Sidi Ahmed ou Moussa, Agadir; marriage festival, Imilchil; *moussem* of Moulay Idris I, Moulay Idris.

October Date festival, Erfoud; music festival, Essaouira.

December Olive festival, Rhafsaï, in the Rif.

A traditional headdress from the Atlas Mountains

WEDDINGS

Moroccan marriages are times of collective celebration, when whole towns join in the rituals that precede the wedding. Traditionally, the father selected a bride for his son. The son had an opportunity to see the chosen girl, at a distance, to express his opinion. All being well, the father then offered the bride's family a dowry. If accepted, this led to an engagement of one to two years. The engagement is a legal part of the marriage process, committing the couple to each other, and permits them to sleep with each other if they so wish.

An urban wedding between wealthy families might last a week, with each day designated for a different ritual. In poorer, rural areas, the wedding often lasts a single day. Before the wedding, there are still numerous rituals that must be followed. After the allotted period of preparation the bride is carried to the bridegroom's house, and there is music, dancing and general uproar. She enters the bridal chamber and the guests settle down to a large meal with further music and dancing. In traditional Berber weddings, the bride is brought to the bridegroom's house on a horse, and then hidden in an upstairs room curtained with carpets so only close family may peek in. The bridegroom must ascend a wooden ladder to reach her.

As in all domains of Moroccan life, the marriage process has been changing rapidly. In cities women now have as much say in the choice of their partner as their Western counterparts. Dowries are no longer an issue: dual incomes, mortgages and tax benefits are more important considerations than gold or camels.

Moroccan women

In the Islamic world, there is no more complicated issue than its treatment of women. There are a lot of misconceptions about Islam and the teachings of the Prophet in the Koran.

Many Islamic teachers argue that the Koran implies that men and women are equal in the eyes of God, and that it is impossible to justify the maltreatment of women based on Islamic law. These teachers even claim that women are given more rights if

Islamic tradition demands that women be covered in public

the Koran is interpreted literally, as they do not have to pray as much as men. They are excused from prayer duties when they are pregnant or menstruating. Likewise during Ramadan, exceptions are made for women who are pregnant or breastfeeding.

Some fundamentalists would have a more stringent interpretation of the Koran. Extremists even view women as evil temptresses, and believe that an unveiled woman not covered from head to toe in full burkha may as well be naked. In some instances women have been attacked for wearing Western dress.

There seems to be no clear uniformity in these interpretations, but it is a fact that women are treated differently in most Islamic nations and don't have what most people in the West would term full human rights. Much of the Western world criticises Islamic nations for this.

Cruelty still meted out to women in extreme Islamic societies includes female infanticide, and stonings and mutilations for even minor misdemeanours. Cultural defence of the way women are treated in these societies, including child marriages, forced purdah (extreme restrictions from social and economic activities) and keeping them uneducated, is in conflict with proper ethical values and human rights in our modern age. The Islamic world is changing and Morocco is at the forefront of this liberalist change and is in transition with respect to how women are treated in society. Perhaps the close proximity to Europe, the internet and satellite television will accelerate the attainment of the equality they deserve.

'A woman is like an apricot – 18 days and she is out of season' is an old Moroccan proverb. It reveals much about the traditional views that a woman exists to serve her husband as long as she is useful to him. The Family Law introduced in 2004 in Morocco changed the balance of this significantly. It is no longer so easy to divorce a woman and to take all of her money, as she is now entitled to an equal share of assets. The legal age of marital consent has been raised to 18 years of age.

Today's generation of young Moroccan women are the first to fight for equal rights in male-dominated areas. The veil is dropping. In the streets of big cities you will see women in Western dress, riding motorbikes, going to work. Birth control is now widely available and birth rates have halved. There is now the same number of boys and girls in

Times are changing. In Casablanca, Islamic dress codes are challenged by Western fashion

secondary education. Government representation is still very low though.

There are still male bastions, such as city cafés, and a pervasive sexist attitude to the roles women can play in business, but these still exist in Western societies, too. In the countryside life is still hard – women do much of the physical labour, which grants them some economic power but leaves them under male control. Girls still leave school at the age of 12 and marry in their teens, to men often 10 years older than them. Things still need to change in Morocco before women gain equality, but at least they are moving in the right direction.

Politics

One of the world's oldest states, Morocco has a continuous 1,200-year history as a single political entity. Moroccans are proud of their distinctiveness, of their historical empires that stretched across North Africa and into Spain. Moroccans have had little say in running their country, controlled by omnipotent sultans. Popular opinion, however, was a great force in obtaining independence, and through the Alaouite dynasty (continued by the current king) a more democratic society has been created.

Background

The first democratic elections were held in 1993. The general public votes to elect the Chamber of Representatives or lower house of the Moroccan Parliament. The Chamber of Counsellors or upper house is elected by local councils, professional bodies and labour unions. The government is headed by the Prime Minister (appointed by the king, who retains supreme authority).

Government

In the September 2007 elections, the Istiqlal (Independence) Party won the most votes, but the government is run by a coalition of four parties. Abbas el Fassi of the Istiqlal Party was appointed Prime Minister by Mohammed VI.

Political issues

In the earliest years of his monarchy, Mohammed VI adopted a policy of social and political reform. His efforts to reduce poverty, improve women's rights and introduce greater press freedom were rightly lauded in the Western world. He seemed to be balancing social reform, while keeping traditionalists happy at the same time.

Then came the 11 September tragedy in 2001 and all in the world changed. A Moroccan was implicated in the planning of the attacks on New York and Washington and put on trial. He was convicted but had his sentence overturned in 2004.

Elections were held in Morocco a year later. To try to stem the rise in Islamic extremism in the country, the Islamic fundamentalist party Justice and Charity was banned from taking part in the elections and its controversial leader, Abdessalam Yassine was temporarily imprisoned. Some government critics claimed this impinged on the legitimacy of the elections and that this party would have polled largest of the Islamic parties, as it has considerable grass roots support. The appointment of Driss Jettou as

Prime Minister, although he was a successful businessman and negotiator, was seen by several commentators as a throwback to the old regime where corruption and mistrust were rife.

Moroccan terrorists allegedly associated with the extremist group Al-Qaeda were implicated in attacks on Casablanca in 2003 and Madrid in 2004. This caused the Moroccan government embarrassment and it has tried to crack down on those associated with extremism.

The Iraq War put a strain on the good trade relations between Morocco and the USA. But most Moroccans are not too interested in Iraq, although they do fear for the fate of their Sunni cousins. Of greater interest perhaps to Moroccans is the Israeli–Palestinian conflict. Even though historically there has been a considerable Jewish population in Morocco, the vast majority of Moroccans would like the conflict resolved in favour of the Palestinian cause.

There are, of course, many other problems besetting a country seeking to modernise. There is a great disparity in riches and a concentration of wealth and industry in the Rabat–Casablanca area to the detriment of the countryside. The birth rate is still high and unemployment is at about 20 per cent. Prices for Morocco's main exports of phosphates and sardines have dropped. But tourism is doing very well and this is the way forward for the Moroccan economy, if the country can stem the tide of intellectual emigration and extremists can be kept at bay.

The Parliament building in Rabat, seat of the 353-member legislature

The royal family

The 15th ruler of the Alaouite dynasty, Mohammed VI, claims direct descent from the Prophet Muhammad and thus is a divine as well as regal leader of Morocco. He is not only a political figurehead but also 'Amir al-Muminin' – 'Commander of the Faithful', the spiritual leader of Islamic Morocco. He continues the Alaouite dynasty, but is a different kind of ruler from his predecessors. His father, Hassan II, 'groomed his son for the throne', but would be shocked at the liberal policies adopted almost immediately by the young king.

Mohammed VI was 35 years of age when he became king and he inherited a peaceful country, but one in which fear and restriction were among the major tenets of rule. Dissension and unpatriotic acts were punished severely.

There is no doubt that, before he became king, Mohammed VI was considered a harmless and disinterested playboy. Few expected the decisiveness of his actions.

Just after his coronation, political prisoners were released from secret jails, a liberal economy was encouraged and restrictions on the press were lifted. He became the champion of the poor and even drove himself about in his own car.

Mohammed VI is revered by his people just as his father was before him. Every shop, business, home and taxi carries his picture, and each public appearance is greeted by cheering crowds. This is no forced popularity: he is loved by his people, many of whom believe that without his unifying influence Morocco would not survive.

The greatest threat to the king's rule is the rise in Islamic fundamentalist extremism in Morocco. Although Moroccans have been implicated in attacks that have been alleged to be by Islamic terrorist groups, the vast majority of Sunni Muslims in the country are non-violent. There is a minority that resort to violence though, and terrorist attacks in Casablanca in 2003 forced the king's hand. He has adopted stringent anti-terror legislation and launched a campaign against extremists, which has been criticised by some commentators as eroding human rights.

By improving the lot of women in Morocco, Mohammed VI has offended many traditionalist Islamic leaders. In 2003, during Ramadan, the first woman Islamic scholar gave a traditional formal presentation in front of the king. This would have been unimaginable during his father's rule. It is a fine line he must tread, trying to balance those who have traditionalist ideals while liberalising the country.

Perhaps the bravest political move made by Mohammed VI has been the new Family Law, which gives women greater rights than men in a divorce settlement. King Mohammed VI has one child who is heir to the throne, Crown Prince Moulay Hassan.

A royal guard at the Tour Hassan in Rabat

Impressions

'How much?' is Morocco's number-one question. Haggling is a way of life here, and no visit is complete without attempting to bargain with a merchant in a medina souk. The process is simple. You decide how much you're willing to pay for something. You are quoted an elevated price – commonly three times what it is actually worth. You express incredulity and offer a price 20–30 per cent below what you want to pay. The merchant ridicules your ignorance. So it continues until you both agree on a price.

Centres Artisanals display official fixed prices for crafts in each city. Use these as a guideline for bargaining. In food markets items are a fixed price, and attempts at haggling may be seen as insulting. Remember that whatever your economic situation you are perceived by locals as wealthy, and compared with them, in most cases, you are.

Culture differences

Many Moroccans, especially in the countryside, are deeply religious. Women who wear veils to preserve themselves from public view are unlikely to appreciate being photographed. Always ask before taking someone's picture. Often you will be asked for money in return: in the case of the colourful snake-charmers and water-sellers of Marrakech this is entirely justifiable – you are paying for a performance as if you were at the theatre or a concert. However, it is unwise to give money to young children: a child who can earn as much as an adult in a day just from smiling at visitors is unlikely to be pushed to go to school. In some areas 50 per cent of the population is still illiterate, and while literacy rates are improving, paying children for photographs is far from constructive.

The Moroccan spirit

The chaotic, colourful life of Moroccan cities has been fixed for centuries and it is unlikely to become more organised, punctual and subdued overnight. At times it might be necessary to adopt the local philosophy of *inshallah* (*see p14*) and go with the flow of things.

While Morocco remains a mysterious country to many outsiders, so the outside world is unknown to many rural Moroccans, who see foreigners only through imported television shows. Satellite TV and the internet make curious urban Moroccans much more aware of international events. Offers of friendship are often genuine and present a fascinating insight into everyday life, but there are always those who see foreigners as little more than walking wallets (*see below*). Your visit is as much a two-way education as an enjoyable and fascinating holiday.

Guides

Official guides are available at all tourist offices and are indispensable – getting round a maze-like medina without them is practically impossible. They are recognisable by their metal 'sheriff's badges' and work on official rates per half and full day. Agree on your itinerary beforehand using the sights described in this book: if you are not interested in shopping, state this firmly – many guides receive large commissions from shopkeepers on tourist purchases and your guide might show undue enthusiasm for getting you into certain boutiques.

Everywhere you go in Morocco, you will be approached by unofficial or *faux* guides. Some claim to be students, but many are just after your money; hardly surprising, in places where one in three men are out of work. Hustlers are best ignored: remain polite, as anger is seen as weakness in the prey. A good way to dispense with unwanted company is not to answer at all. The individual soon gets bored and moves on to fresher pastures. In the event of any trouble find the nearest policeman – hustlers immediately vanish. A sure way to avoid unpleasantness is always to hire an official guide.

Islam

Understanding Morocco is impossible without an understanding of Islam. Islam means 'submission', a term which suggests the all-pervading influence of the religion in Moroccan society. Moroccan law is Islamic law; the king is Commander of the Faithful.

Islam was founded by Muhammad, a merchant from Mecca who became Allah's prophet in AD 610. 'Allah' is the same God as worshipped by Christians and Jews, and for Muslims Jesus Christ is a prophet like Muhammad but not God's son, since God is one, not a Holy Trinity. Islam is unique in denying an

Traditional Arabic temple in Marrakech

The entrance to the shrine of Moulay Idris II, who developed Fès

intermediary between God and humankind – there are no priests as such and no liturgy. Prayer is a direct relationship between the faithful and God. The Holy Book, or Koran, was revealed directly from God via the Prophet Muhammad, and combines much of the philosophy of Christianity and Judaism.

Islam is built on five pillars or duties: *chahada*, the profession that 'there is no god but God and Muhammad is the prophet of God'; *salat*, prayer five times a day; *zakat*, the giving of alms to the poor; Ramadan, the month-long fast; and *hadj*, the pilgrimage to Mecca.

Sunni, Shiite and Sufi

After Muhammad's death the Islamic world was thrown into confusion. A schism developed between the Umayyad and Abbasid caliphs, religious leaders chosen to teach the

Koran and follow the practice (*sunna*) of Muhammad, and disciples of Ali, Muhammad's son-in-law (*shi'at Ali* – partisans of Ali). This split led to civil war and in the early 8th century many Shiite refugees, facing persecution in Tunisia and Andalucía, flocked to Morocco. Today, however, the vast majority of Moroccan Muslims are orthodox Sunni, like those in the Middle East. In rural areas religion is less orthodox, based on more mystical beliefs surrounding local holy men or saints. Such Islamic mysticism is known as Sufism, and the continuing influence of 'Sufi' brotherhoods, or *Zaiouas*, is felt throughout rural Morocco. Festivals celebrating local Sufi saints are attended by huge crowds.

Prayer

In every settlement there is a mosque (*jemma* in Arabic) from which the call to prayer is sung daily by the *muezzin* (chosen person who leads the call to prayer). Prayers take place at dawn, noon, mid-afternoon, dusk and before sleep. The faithful prostrate themselves towards Mecca, the direction indicated by the mosque prayer niche (*mihrab*). Friday is the Islamic holy day when a congregational prayer is offered at noon (most businesses close by 11.30am). In Morocco entry to nearly all mosques is prohibited to non-Muslims.

Ramadan

The month of Ramadan varies each year, as it follows the ninth month in the Islamic lunar calendar (*Kijri*) when the Koran was revealed to Muhammad. It is always a time of strict fasting, during which the faithful abstain from food, cigarettes and any sexual contact from dawn until dusk. At nightfall the streets erupt, shops and restaurants open their doors and festivities carry on well into the small hours. Before sunrise a last meal is taken, the fast recommencing when, as the Koran states, 'one can distinguish a white from a black thread'. The only exemptions from the fast are younger children, pregnant women, the old and sick, and travellers on long journeys. Other Muslims found disobeying the fast are liable to punishment by the authorities. Non-Muslims are free to eat and drink what they like, but moderation from tourists is appreciated. Given the extreme climate in parts of Morocco, especially in summer, the Ramadan fast is a serious undertaking and a time of great introspection.

Inside the Hassan II Mosque, Casablanca

Moroccan Islam

Morocco has always been different. Morocco's founder, Moulay Idris, was a Shiite refugee from the Islamic civil war in Baghdad. While today nearly all Moroccans are orthodox Sunnis, like most Muslims in the Middle East, the remoteness of much of the country's people has led to an interesting blend of Islamic practices and popular spiritualism. Diversity is still the rule, not the exception. Marabouts, tombs of the righteous, dot the Moroccan countryside and are revered as places of great power, where women seek fertility, the sick good health and everyone else good luck. It is unwise for non-Muslims to approach too closely, as these tombs are held in great awe by locals.

Language

Moroccans are renowned linguists. French is spoken almost everywhere and many Moroccans are bilingual Arabic-French. In much of the north the second language is Spanish. English is spoken by young people and in major tourist resorts, but in remoter countryside French is essential. Many signposts are purely in Arabic.

Moroccan Arabic is very different from the classical Arabic spoken in the Middle East. Learning to count would be useful for bargaining purposes and a few common words will always amuse your listeners (*see p183*). Berber dialects are also spoken by 40 per cent of the population, in the Rif mountains, the Atlas ranges and the south.

Kif

Kif, hashish and chocolaté are all terms for cannabis resin, sold in brown cubes or in *majoun* jam. Cultivated in the isolated valleys of the Rif, kif is big business and, as a banned narcotic, illegal. Traditionally, the smoking of kif has been a pastime for Moroccans and tourists alike, but as Moroccan officials state, just the possession of cannabis is enough to incur a three-month to five-year prison sentence. Many dealers also work as informers to the police, and embassies in Rabat carry thick files of foreigners now languishing in Moroccan jails. To be safe, avoid the kif-growing areas in the Rif around Ketama. Picking up hitchhikers is also ill-advised: if one member of a car is found to possess kif, everyone in the car is arrested.

Itineraries

The diversity of Morocco makes it an ideal place for touring. Hiring a car is highly recommended – distances are large, but quickly covered under one's own steam, and you can see much of the country in two weeks. Public transport is plentiful but time-consuming, and for remoter sights, especially in the Haut Atlas (High Atlas), a car is essential. Most international hire companies allow you to pick up a car from one airport and return it to another (*see p180*).

The north

A popular summer circuit, the north offers the Atlantic beaches of Asilah and Larache, and the exotic port of Tanger.

Families often head to the quiet, unspoilt Mediterranean coastline, while the more adventurous climb to the white towns of Tetouan and Chefchaouen and into the wild mountains of the Rif. Many visitors combine a week here with a week visiting the imperial cities and the south.

The imperial cities

The four imperial capitals of Morocco provide a fascinating journey from the southern gateway of Marrakech to Fès and Meknès, and across to the majestic Atlantic capital of Rabat. This itinerary includes excursions into the High Atlas, the cedar forests of the Moyen Atlas (Middle Atlas), the ancient Roman city of Volubilis and the Muslim holy town of Moulay Idris. Once at the coast, upmarket beach resorts such as Mohammedia, Temara and Skhirat offer restful stretches of sand. When planning your trip, remember Marrakech is very hot in summer – spring and early autumn are good times to visit. In winter months the passes of the High Atlas from Marrakech to Fès may sometimes be closed due to bad weather.

The south

For many visitors, the south is the highlight of a trip to Morocco. Here, as the High Atlas gives way to arid valleys and lush oases, is African Morocco. Camels graze the riverbeds of the Dra and Ziz valleys, while at Erfoud 150m (490ft) high sand dunes rise into a blue sky. Dates are the region's main crop –

millions of palm trees carpet the otherwise barren land. On the coast, Agadir is a modern resort offering excellent leisure facilities. Further north, Essaouira is a more traditional coastal town with a bustling fishing port and enchanting beaches. High season in the south is from September to May, when temperatures regularly exceed 40°C (104°F).

Safety

Crime rates in Morocco are quite low, but care is advised in big cities where petty theft and pickpocketing are common. Women should be careful when travelling alone – strict restraints on local women, combined with widespread Westernised pornography, mean Moroccan men have a sadly distorted view of the 'availability' of Western females.

In the event of hassle, engage the help of passers-by – shouting '*chouma*' or 'shame' often does the trick. Most Moroccans will come to your aid if they see you are in trouble. If you find yourself with an overpersistent 'guide', head for a policeman – such insistent bothering of tourists is illegal and the tout will soon vanish.

There have been no recent terrorist attacks in Morocco (at time of writing). However, it is labelled as a country with a heightened risk of international terrorism, so be vigilant especially in hotels and restaurants.

It is now safe to travel to Western Sahara, following peace accords signed with Polisario rebels. Otherwise, as mentioned, it is best to avoid the remoter areas of the Rif, where kif cultivation is still prevalent.

What to wear

Modest dress is required away from international resorts. Covering of legs and arms is advised for both men and women. Topless sunbathing is rare, mainly confined to the beaches of Agadir. In winter it can get very cold, even in the south when night-time temperatures plunge. The same applies to the High Atlas in summer, where warm clothing is recommended, as nights and early mornings are cold. Contrary to popular belief, it does rain in Morocco, especially in the north (the Rif receives 2,000mm/79in of rain a year) so waterproof clothing is useful in autumn and winter. Sturdy shoes are advisable for the south and boots are necessary for Atlas hiking (*see p136*).

Setting out from the grandiose city walls of Rabat

Impressions

The north

The Straits of Gibraltar, the legendary pillars of Hercules, are all that separate northern Morocco from Europe. This wild land of green mountains, towering cliffs and deserted beaches seems a world away from the arid expanses of Morocco to the south. The northern coastline, once inaccessible and underdeveloped, is rapidly becoming one of Morocco's most popular destinations, prized for its clear waters and Mediterranean climate.

Inland, foothills rise to jagged peaks, while whitewashed villages huddle in fertile valleys. In contrast, the great port of Tanger is a growing metropolis offering modern facilities and a cosmopolitan atmosphere. Further east, Oujda stands on the border with Algeria, a thoroughly Arab city.

The north of Morocco is a region used to visitors. The Phoenicians settled here in 1100 BC, followed by the Romans. Moulay Idris, founder of Morocco, first set foot on Moroccan soil at Tanger in AD 788. Later came Portuguese traders, then Muslim and Jewish refugees from the Inquisition in 15th-century Spain. In 1661 the English moved into Tanger, only to be kicked out by Moulay Ismaïl in 1684 (their withdrawal was orchestrated by Lord Dartmouth, assisted by diarist Samuel Pepys, who admitted a 'loathing' for the port). In 1777 American ships were permitted to dock in Tanger, making Morocco the first country to recognise the new United States.

The north has always been a melting pot for different races, cultures and nationalities. Even today Spain holds two towns along this north coast – the enclaves of Ceuta and Melilla – and Spanish is still spoken in Tetouan and Chefchaouen.

Roads are good along the north coast, but bus services are often crowded. It is advisable to stick to main roads when driving in the Rif, the centre of kif production, and not to stop for hitchhikers or fake 'accidents'.

Welcome to Africa – the entrance to the Caves of Hercules, Tanger

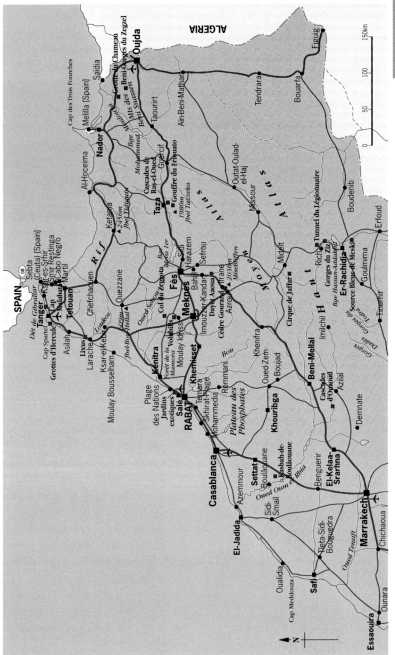

TANGER (TANGIER)

Romans, Arabs, Portuguese, English and French have all sought to possess the enigmatic beauty and strategic position of Tanger, the 'queen' of the Mediterranean. Within sight of Europe, washed by Atlantic waves, Tanger was once known as the world's most international city.

The city's history is as turbulent as its seas, continually swept by tides of Western and Eastern invaders. From the days of Rome to the infamous 'international zone' of this century, Tanger has been a city apart from the rest of Morocco. In its jet-setting heyday, anything went; it was said there was nothing one could not buy in its smoky bars and seedy souks. Artists and writers flocked from America and Europe, drawn to the bohemian lifestyle. It was also a haven for the stylish, affluent 'Mediterranean set', film stars and the criminal underworld.

Today's Tanger is calm – a modern port, with a large tourist trade. Many of the insalubrious nightspots and seedy dens of iniquity are closed. Sparkling apartment blocks sprout daily. Further speculation talks of a tunnel or bridge connecting Morocco with Spain in the future.

Guides available from Tourist Office, 29 boulevard Pasteur. Tel: (039) 94 80 50.

Avenue des FAR

Tanger's main hotel strip (its long name is 'avenue des Forces Armée Royale'), bordering the beach, is a wide avenue also containing numerous beach clubs, once enjoyed by playwrights Tennessee Williams and Joe Orton.

Charf

At the highest point of the city, to the south of the bay, the disused mosque on Charf Hill offers the best vantage for an uninterrupted view of Tanger.

Grand Socco (Place 9 Avril 1947)

Not so long ago, warriors from the Rif mountains would ride to the Grand Socco on camels, announcing their arrival with musket shots. Today, the Socco (from souk, meaning 'market') is still lively and Riffians descend to market on Thursday and Sunday. It was in this square, on 9 April 1947, that Sultan Mohammed first called for Morocco's independence from France.

Jardin du Mendoubia

Through a large blue door on the western side of the Grand Socco is the Mendoubia Garden, a rambling haven of greenery containing an immense Dragon Tree, said to be over 800 years old. In its trunk one can make out the twisted figure of a man – the captured spirit, so legend has it, of an evil 13th-century prince.

50 Grand Socco, through the blue gates. Open: daily 9am–noon & 3–6pm (in theory). Admission free (doorman expects a tip).

Kasbah and Dar el Makhzen

The kasbah is one of the most famous landmarks of Tanger, a fortress-like settlement overlooking the port. It was in this collection of rambling white houses that Woolworth heiress Barbara Hutton lived, having outbid General Franco of Spain to buy 'Villa Sidi Hosni', the palace where she held extravagant parties for rich and famous guests. Through Bab el Aissa is the Dar el Makhzen, or Royal Palace, built by Moulay Ismaïl to celebrate the English departure from Tanger; it now houses an interesting museum. Exhibits include remains from local Roman sites, pottery, rugs and a bone said to come from Jonah's whale. Most pleasant of all are the Andalusian gardens, aromatic and shady, from where a gate leads to the Belvédère.

Northeast of the medina, follow rue Ben Raisouli to place Amrah. Kasbah Museum, place de la Kasbah. Tel: (039) 93 20 97. Open: Wed–Mon 9am–4.30pm. Admission charge.

La Légation des États-Unis (American Legation Museum)

Donated to President Monroe by Sultan Moulay Suleiman in 1821, this is the

The kasbah in Tanger

only US national monument outside the United States. The old consulate now houses local works of art, as well as a collection of immaculate antiques. Symbols of Moroccan–American friendship abound, including a Moroccan rug woven into the stars and stripes, and a 1789 letter from George Washington to the Moroccan sultan. *8 Zankat America. Tel: (039) 93 53 17; fax: (039) 93 59 60. Open: Mon–Fri 10am–1pm & 3–5pm. Admission free.*

La Montagne

When wealthy Europeans first settled in Tanger they built their villas on the wooded Montagne, or mountain, to the west of the port. Now a dense conglomeration of extravagant mansions, it offers a pleasant antidote to the prosaic chaos of the medina: follow directions to the Country Club to view The People's Dispensary for Sick Animals Rest Home, the most curious cemetery in the city.

The sea gate in the kasbah walls of Tanger

Medina and Petit Socco

Smaller than many Moroccan medinas, the Tanger version is as animated and spicy as any (look after cameras and money as you walk). Rue es Siaghin was traditionally the jewellers' street, run by Jewish craftsmen, but now sells a cornucopia of Westernised junk. This leads to the Petit Socco, the heart of the medina and, some would say, of Tanger – a ramshackle huddle of cafés where, in bygone days, you could have bumped into Errol Flynn, Cary Grant and Henri Matisse. Today the clientele has seen better days, but an hour spent in the Café Central will provide many a story.

Musée d'Art Moderne

Housed in the former British Consulate, this exhibition of modern Moroccan art is both colourful and entertaining. It includes one painting by a former communications minister showing a chaotic tangle of wires, as well as vibrant symbolist work from the Asilah school.
52 rue d'Angleterre. Tel: (039) 94 99 72. Open: 9am–4.30pm. Closed: Tue. Admission charge.

Palais Mendoub (Forbes Museum)

Malcolm Forbes bought this coastal palace in 1970 as a retreat and museum for his vast collection of toy soldiers.
Avenue Mohammed Tazi, Marshan district. Tel: (039) 93 36 06; fax: (039) 93 43 28. Open: 10am–4pm. Closed: Thur. Admission free.

The American Legation in Tanger

Place de France

Hub of international Tanger, place de France once rivalled the Grand and Petit Soccos as a centre of political and literary gossip. Artists, politicians, actors and smugglers mingled daily at the Café de Paris. Opposite, the imposing French Consulate is a reminder of colonial splendour. Next door, the French cultural centre – Galerie Delacroix – holds sporadic exhibitions.
Galerie Delacroix, rue de la Liberté. Tel: (039) 94 10 54. Open: daily 9am–noon & 3–6pm. Admission free.

Sunset over the Atlantic and the Cap Spartel lighthouse

TANGER ENVIRONS
Cap Malabata and Ksar-es-Srhir

The long sweep of the Bay of Tanger is guarded by two impressive promontories. To the east, Cap Malabata and its 19th-century lighthouse guard the entrance to the Mediterranean, offering views back to Tanger and across to Algeciras in Spain. From the lighthouse rough tracks lead along pine-clad cliffs and down to small, unspoilt beaches. Nearby, a ruined folly provides a suitably dramatic counterpoint.

The road east along the coast is little explored by tourists, although it is one of the prettiest in Morocco. About 33km (21 miles) from Tanger, the small resort of Ksar-es-Srhir is a good base from which to explore sandy coves and dramatic cliff paths. Continuing eastwards the road hugs the sea until the Spanish enclave of Ceuta.

Cap Spartel and Grottes d'Hercule (Cape Spartel and the Caves of Hercules)

Drive 14km (9 miles) past mansions and umbrella pines west of Tanger and you arrive at Cap Spartel and its lighthouse, a twin of that at Cap Malabata. It is a dramatically beautiful spot – the most northwesterly tip of Africa, where the Atlantic meets the Mediterranean. Across the sea to the north lies **Cabo Trafalgar**, site of Lord Nelson's last battle.

Cap Spartel can be desolate in winter, buffeted by Atlantic storms, but in summer the sun shines, the sea is turquoise and the beach, stretching 45km (28 miles) southwards to Asilah, seems the most beautiful in the world (beware of strong currents).

Just to the south, past Robinson Plage, is one of the most remarkable sights in Morocco: the illustrious Caves of Hercules. Accessible by a series of dank steps, these two caves were once temples of a mysterious prehistoric cult (hundreds of Neolithic phalluses were excavated from here in the 1920s). In the international years, bizarreness was the order of the day: a party thrown by photographer Cecil Beaton involved one cave being filled with champagne, the other with hashish. The caves' legendary status comes, however, from their seaward entrance, shaped like an inverse map of Africa. In the evening, this natural 'gateway to Africa' provides an unforgettable frame for the setting sun.

Cap Spartel was much prized by the Romans: below the Caves of Hercules lie the jumbled ruins of **Cotta**, an ancient anchovy port, where the little fish were skinned, pounded and added to olive oil to make *garum*, a popular Roman snack. Just inland are the ruins of the settlement of Ashaka. In Roman times the area was known as Ampelusium, or Cape of Wine. *Caves of Hercules: open daily 8.30am–6pm. Admission charge. Cotta and Ashaka are half-heartedly closed to visitors behind a wire fence.*

The north

SPANISH ENCLAVES

When the Spanish pulled out of Morocco in 1956 they retained two northern ports which remain to this day 'Sovereign Territory of Spain' and part of the EU. Ceuta (Sebta in Arabic), the larger, lies at the northernmost tip of Morocco opposite another enclave, British-held Gibraltar. Ceuta has been heavily fortified since 1580, and there is still a large Spanish military presence. Most visitors come for duty-free shopping – electrical goods, petrol and alcohol – or to catch the ferry. It is a pleasant enough place to wander, especially up to Mont Acho (181m/594ft high), offering a good view of Gibraltar. Further east, Melilla is even less interesting: once an export centre for zinc from the Rif, it now relies on duty-free shoppers. Melilla's administration centre is in Málaga, across the sea, and daily flights connect with Spain. Crossing the border into each enclave is a tedious process. Hire cars are not permitted to make the transition.

Walk: Tanger town

This walk leads through the heart of Tanger and districts made famous by numerous writers and artists, into the colourful maze of the medina and up to the ramparts of the kasbah.

Allow 3 hours.

Begin at the Tourist Office on boulevard Pasteur and continue to place de France.

1 Place de France

This was the meeting place of writers Paul Bowles and William Burroughs, who used to drink at the Café de Paris. A few doors down, El Minzah, a luxurious hotel, served as HQ for spies and agents during World War II.
Follow rue de la Liberté 100m (110yd) then turn left to reach rue d'Angleterre.

2 St Andrew's Church

The focus for the English-speaking community. Walter Harris, the *Times* correspondent, is buried here, as is Emily Keane, who married the Shereef of Ouezzane. He fell in love with her as she combed her hair in a hotel window.
Open: 9.30am–12.30pm & 2.30–6.30pm. Closed: Sat & Sun.
Head between the two lines of palm trees by the bus station to Café Orient and an excellent view over the Grand Socco.

3 Grand Socco

The market in the corner offers vegetables, fruit and spices (including aphrodisiacs). The fish market sells everything from shrimps to sharks. Look out for women from the Rif mountains dressed in their distinctive sombrero hats and red and white striped skirts.
Descend rue es Siaghin, on the north side of the Grand Socco, to the Petit Socco.

4 Petit Socco

Once the Roman Forum, in bygone days the square was a place of illicit deals. It still retains a decrepit charm.
Take rue des Almohades to place Ouad Ahardane. From here, rue Ben Raisouli leads to the kasbah.

5 The souks

Wander past displays of leather, copperware, pottery and carpets. The prices here are likely to be higher than elsewhere, but it is fun to bargain. There are also natural beauty products, including perfume made from goats' dung and lipstick derived from mud!
Take rue Ben Raisouli to place Amrah. Just below here is Villa Sidi Hosni.

6 Villa Sidi Hosni

Behind these simple white walls was the home of the 'Queen of the Medina', Barbara Woolworth Hutton, who lived here until her death in 1979. Its lavish decorations included 30 gold clocks and a $1 million dollar Indian tapestry encrusted with jewels. Villa Sidi Hosni is closed to the public.

From place Amrah pass through Bab el Aissa into the kasbah.

7 The kasbah and Belvédère

Inhabited since the Middle Ages, many of the present walls date from Moulay Ismaïl's 18th-century building spree. Place de la Kasbah was the site of public executions until the 1800s. From the Belvédère there is a memorable view over the bay.

Take rue de la Kasbah through the gateway to Bab Fahs. From here take a taxi back into town.

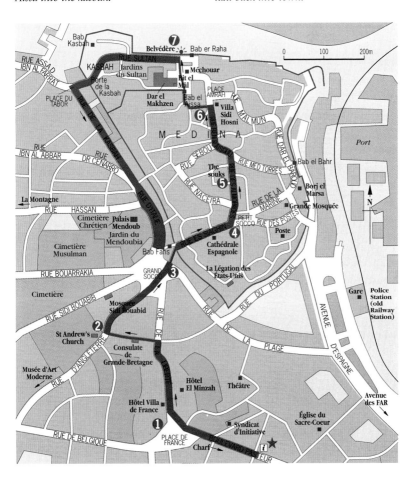

Writers and artists

Be it beautiful light, exotic inspiration, inexpensive living or liberal laws concerning drugs and homosexuality – whatever the reason, Morocco can claim to have inspired some of the world's greatest writers and artists.

European artists flocked here seeking to discover the Orient and its

Villa Sidi Hosni, venue for 1920s jet-set parties

exotic secrets. One of the first was French painter Eugène Delacroix, who accompanied a French delegation in 1832. Matisse spent two summers in Tanger, while fauvist Raoul Dufy visited Marrakech. They became quickly addicted to the colours, light and lifestyle: as Matisse exclaimed, 'Tanger, Tanger, I wish I had the courage to get out of here.'

But it was the American writers of the 1930s, 1940s and 1950s who put Morocco firmly on the cultural map. One of the first was Paul Bowles, a young composer from New York who arrived in Tanger with Aaron Copland in 1931. Author of *The Sheltering Sky*, in which three Americans travel into the Sahara on a voyage of self-discovery, Bowles was at the centre of a literary pilgrimage which brought the likes of Tennessee Williams, Truman Capote and 'beatnik' writers Jack Kerouac, Allen Ginsberg and William S Burroughs to Tanger. Burroughs was so fascinated by the city that he used it as his inspiration for Interzone, the nightmarish world described in his novel *Naked Lunch*. British playwright Joe Orton was a regular visitor until his death in 1967.

Morocco has also attracted film-makers, drawn by guaranteed good weather, low production costs and spectacular settings. Orson Welles

The tomb of Walter Harris, the *Times* correspondent to Morocco

filmed much of his *Othello* in Essaouira as early as 1949, and David Lean's *Lawrence of Arabia* was mostly shot near Ouarzazate. So great is Hollywood's interest in Morocco that Ouarzazate now boasts its own film studios, where James Bond films have been made, as well as *Jewel of the Nile* and Scorsese's *Last Temptation of Christ*.

THE NORTHWEST COAST

Asilah is a pretty, whitewashed port on the Atlantic coast, and makes a relaxing change from city bustle. The small streets recall Grecian villages, while wrought-iron balconies show a Spanish influence. In August the town hosts an International Festival of Music and Culture, attracting artists from around the world. Colourful murals are drawn on the walls of the city as part of the festival.

The easy-going atmosphere belies a tumultuous past: first a Phoenician fishing port, then Roman Silis, Asilah subsequently attracted the Portuguese, who needed a loading point for gold from Timbuktu. In 1471 they sent an armada of some 500 ships and 30,000 men, who eventually captured the town and constructed sea battlements which survive today.

The palace of Er Raisuli (*see box*) is not strictly open to the public, but you might be able to get in to have a look. Three huge gates lead into the medina – the most impressive, **Bab Homar** (down from the palace), still bears the Portuguese coat of arms. In contrast, colourful pop-art murals painted by festival artists adorn many of the whitewashed walls. To the north, the long sandy beach attracts legions of summer tourists.

46km (29 miles) south of Tanger, 232km (144 miles) north of Rabat. Accessible by road or rail (five trains a day to Tanger or Casablanca). Souk: Thur.

Larache

Larache is less visited and more welcoming than Asilah. This was the main port for the Spanish-occupied north until 1956 and Spanish signs still decorate shops and hotels. There is even a small Spanish cathedral. French writer Jean Genet lived here and is buried in the cemetery on the road to Tanger. Today, Larache makes its living from tuna fishing and meagre tourism.

There are few sights: the large 17th-century Spanish fortress, **Château de la Cigogne** (Stork Castle), offers a fine sea view (storks nest here from April to September; the ruins are intermittently open – a guide can usually be found), and **place de la Libération** dates from the Spanish era. From this central square a red and white gate leads into the small medina – far from tourist-oriented, and a good place for bargains.

In summer Larache is busy with Moroccan tourists enjoying the huge

ER RAISULI

Asilah's most infamous resident was a flamboyant bandit named Er Raisuli, who specialised in kidnapping at the turn of the 20th century. President Roosevelt bailed out one victim, Greek-American millionaire Perdicaris; the *Times* correspondent Walter Harris was chained to a headless corpse in Raisuli's dungeons. Adversaries were often made to walk the plank from his seaside palace. 'Your justice is great, but these rocks are more merciful,' shouted one victim as he jumped. Raisuli subsequently became governor of northern Morocco, until his imprisonment and death in 1925.

beach to the north, one of the best and safest along this coast.

87km (54 miles) south of Tanger, 191km (119 miles) north of Rabat.

Lixus

Most foreign tourists to Larache come to see the Roman ruins of Lixus, site of the legendary 'Garden of Hesperides', where Hercules picked golden apples after killing the local dragon (local tangerines are said to be the source of the legend). Founded in 1000 BC by the Phoenicians, Lixus was Roman until the 5th century AD, a thriving port dedicated to *garum*, or anchovy paste production. The ruined factories are still visible, along with a theatre/amphitheatre which specialised in wild animal combats. The remains of the baths contain a mosaic depicting Neptune, but most relics were removed to the museum in Tetouan.

5km (3 miles) northeast of Larache, accessible by car, bus or chartered rowing boat. Open: daily, sunrise to sunset. Admission free.

Moulay Bousselham

This small beach resort is famous for its lagoon, a reserve specialising in flamingos. To the northeast is Arbaoua hunting reserve, open to lovers of snipe-shooting.

86km (53 miles) south of Larache.

Whitewashed houses and Portuguese ramparts at Asilah, one of Morocco's prettiest ports

THE RIF

The chain of spectacular mountains, stretching 300km (186 miles) to the Algerian border, is traditionally the wildest place in Morocco – the Bled es Siba, or 'ungovernable land'. Riffian tribes have always been fiercely independent: prospective conquerors, from Romans to a succession of Moroccan sultans, have consistently failed to gain a foothold in this barren landscape.

Historically the Rif has been the centre of kif production, the Indian hemp grown to extract marijuana. Be cautious, especially around the town of Ketama, the headquarters for this illicit trade: do not stop on the road (ignore hitch-hikers, or apparent 'accidents'), and decline any dubious offers to visit 'farms'.

Morocco remains one of the world's largest producers and exporters of cannabis, even though government initiatives during the last six years have led to a 10–45 per cent fall in cannabis production in the Rif.

Tourism is seen as a replacement industry and the beautiful Mediterranean coastline is under development, and many of the smaller towns and villages are being 'discovered' for the first time. This region was Spanish until 1956, and the architecture and ambience are Andalusian. Towns like Tetouan, Chefchaouen and the eastern border city of Oujda welcome tourists with traditions and history far removed from those of central and southern Morocco.

Al-Hoceima

The biggest resort on the Mediterranean coast, Al-Hoceima enjoys a dramatic setting – a huge bay backed by cliffs, enclosing a magnificent white sand beach. The small fishing village has been overtaken by tourist developments which welcome mainly French package holidaymakers. Three islands lie offshore, all Spanish owned, including **Peñon de Alhuceimas**, an ancient fortress prison. Since 1990 Al-Hoceima has been at the epicentre of two earthquakes. The bigger one was in February 2004 and measured 6.5 on the Richter scale, killing 572 people. Most buildings are built to withstand the effects of a major quake. However, do read any emergency instructions on what to do in the event of an earthquake. Most hotels will have them displayed in the rooms or have them up in reception.

327km (203 miles) east of Tanger, 293km (182 miles) west of Oujda.

Chefchaouen

This exquisite mountain town makes an attractive alternative base to Tetouan. Founded by Muslims and Jews fleeing the 15th-century Inquisition in Andalucía, Chefchaouen had been entered by only three Western visitors until the Spanish defeated the great Riffian leader Abd el Krim in 1920 (the illustrious trio comprised a journalist, a cartographer disguised as a rabbi and a missionary who was poisoned for his trouble). When they finally broke through, Spanish soldiers discovered people speaking Andalusian dialects extinct in Spain for over 400 years.

Today, the town is famous for its houses painted in bright white and blue (rumoured to dispel mosquitoes), and its impressive setting beneath the twin peaks of Jbel Chaouen (Chaouen means 'the horns' in Berber).

Chefchaouen's medina is one of the prettiest and most welcoming in Morocco, dazzlingly white in the morning sun and embellished with arches, wrought-iron balconies and delicate stucco. The town is the weaving capital of the region, with 1,500 looms. Wool is brought down from the mountains to be woven into *jellabah* (traditional Arabic robes): each village has its own distinctive *jellabah* design, rather like clan kilts in Scotland.

On place Outa el Hammam is the kasbah fortress of **Abd el Krim**, intermittently open to the public. Inside the prisons, where the Berber leader was kept chained by the Spanish, neck, arm and foot irons still hang from the damp walls.

61km (38 miles) south of Tetouan, 118km (73 miles) southeast of Tanger. Souk: Mon & Thur.

The valleys of the Rif are rich producers of olives and corn as well as cannabis

Ketama

At the heart of the Rif, Ketama was once a popular mountain resort, with tourists coming to ski and hunt on the slopes of neighbouring Jbel Tidiquin, at 2,456m (8,058ft) the highest of the Riffian mountains. Today, however, it is more notorious as the capital of kif production, and caution is advised; locals are unlikely to believe you are here for more innocent pleasures.

112km (70 miles) east of Chefchaouen, 107km (66 miles) west of Al-Hoceima.

MONTS DES BENI SNASSEN (Beni Snassen Mountains)

This fertile eastern limb of the Rif contains two popular and impressive diversions: the large **Grotte du Chameau** (Camel's Cave) – a cavern of spiky stalactites (bring a torch), and the nearby **Beni-Gorges du Zegzel** (Zegel Gorge) – a dramatic limestone fault.

90km (56 miles) west of Oujda.

Ouezzane

This is olive country, a fruit full of *baraka*, or divine blessing, for Moroccans – Ouezzane's 600,000 olive trees produce the finest oil in Morocco. A pretty sprawl of white houses covering the slopes of Jbel-Bou-Hellal, Ouezzane traditionally marked the boundary between the Bled el Makhzen and Bled es Siba, the governed and lawless lands. It was ruled by Idrisid Shereefs, holy men who claimed ancestry from the Prophet Muhammad.

Today the cobbled streets offer glimpses of country life that has changed little over the centuries.

60km (37 miles) southwest of Chefchaouen. Souk: Thur.

Oujda

Capital of eastern Morocco, Oujda lies in the Angad plain on the border with Algeria. It is surprisingly fertile, with oases and floral avenues nourished by mountain streams. Historically the city has been a military football, passed between marauding armies since the Zenata tribe settled here in the 10th century. Oujda was the only Moroccan city to become Turkish during Ottoman invasions, and was French longer than anywhere else in the country (from 1907, five years before the Protectorate).

There is little to see in town, although the souks are lively and devoid of tourists. **Bab Abd el Ouahab**, or Gate of the Heads, was the exhibition centre for severed enemy heads in the 17th century. Today it commands a lively square, home to musicians and storytellers.

For verdant relaxation, try **Lalla Aicha park**, to the east of the medina, or the palm oasis of **Sidi Yahya**, 6km (4 miles) south of Oujda, and its sacred marabouts. Legend states that the tomb of Sidi Yahya is actually that of John the Baptist.

609km (378 miles) southeast of Tanger, 343km (213 miles) northeast of Fès. Souk: Sun & Wed.

Saïdia

A developing eastern Mediterranean beach resort, very popular with Moroccans, Saïdia's 15km (9 miles) of sand offer perfect swimming but the crowds are intense in summer.
60km (37 miles) north of Oujda.

Tetouan

Known as 'Daughter of Granada', Tetouan was capital of Spanish Morocco until 1956; its Art Deco buildings are still adorned with Spanish signs and advertising, and many locals still speak fluent Spanish. Tetouan means 'open your eyes' in Berber – wise advice in this intriguing town.

Engage an official guide for the maze of the medina, busy with craftsmen, dyers and tanners. Particularly interesting is **Souk el Houdz**, the Berber market where local women sell red and white striped *foutas*, distinctive Riffian skirts.

From the medina, Bab el Okla (the Queen's Gate) leads to the local **Artisan School**, located in a converted palace. Do not miss a tour around the classrooms: Tetouan is justly renowned for its woodcraft and pottery mosaics. Just inside the medina walls, the small **Folklore Museum** has older works of art, including displays of marriage ceremonies, a Berber kitchen and Jewish jewellery. To the west of the medina, on place el Jala, stands the **Archaeological Museum**, which contains statues and mosaics from Roman Lixus and Volubilis.

57km (35 miles) southeast of Tanger, 281km (175 miles) north of Fès. Official guide from Tourist Office, 30 avenue Mohammed V (tel: (039) 57 78 00; fax: (039) 47 90 02).

Tetouan beaches

The nearest beach to Tetouan is **Martil**, a medieval port now backed by modern boulevards and vast apartment blocks. Further north, the long beach at **Cabo Negro** boasts two tourist complexes, including an 18-hole golf course. The 'Black Cape' itself is unspoilt: wild boar still roam its slopes. Just beyond the small fishing port of M'Diq is **Kabila**, a Spanish-style resort in verdant grounds. **MarinaSmir** is part of the development of Oued Negro, Restinga and Holiday Club. It is the newest addition and comes under the umbrella of Tamuda Bay, a 50ha (124-acre) resort.

Collecting water at place de l'Oussa in the medina of Tetouan

The north

Central plains, Moyen Atlas and the Atlantic coast

Central Morocco is the country's most populated region, with 40 per cent of the population living within 20km (12 miles) of the Atlantic coast. The coastline has seen a dramatic expansion: Casablanca alone has grown to 100 times its size since 1900. Industrial complexes, commuter towns and smart beach resorts connect Casablanca, the business capital, to Rabat, the administrative capital.

Inland, the wide plains are rich in phosphates and other minerals, and support the bulk of Morocco's agriculture – fields of corn, olives, fruit and vines (a legacy of former French occupation). Further east, hills unfold

One of the storage rooms at the old Royal Granary at Meknès (*see pp69–70*)

from the plains, rising towards Fès and the Middle Atlas. Capital of culture, often scathing about its prosaic cousins on the coast, Fès is a city of graceful minarets, towering ruins and medieval streets. Neighbouring Meknès was Morocco's capital in the days of omnipotent sultan Moulay Ismaïl, and its gargantuan walls are among the most impressive in the Arab world.

The Middle Atlas region, stretching southwards from Fès, is a wilder land of mountains and plateaux. Giant cedar forests cover much of the higher hills, where Morocco's native monkey, the Barbary ape, roams wild. Snow covers these slopes in winter, and places like Ifrane are more reminiscent of Alpine resorts than African villages. This is the land of the Berbers: low black tents dot the landscape, while herds of sheep and goats roam the valley pastures. Get off the beaten track into the hills and you will be rewarded with waterfalls, lakes and spectacular rock formations that could be a scene from an old Western.

Archways at Morocco's major landmark, the Hassan II Mosque in Casablanca

CASABLANCA

Those expecting romance and adventure here will be disappointed. Humphrey Bogart never came here, and the film *Casablanca* was shot entirely in Hollywood. 'Casa' is, in fact, Africa's second-largest city after Cairo, with a population estimated between 3 and 4 million (from a mere 20,000 in 1900, before French governor Marshal Lyautey chose it as his administrative capital).

Today, downtown Casablanca is modern and not unlike Western cities, with wide boulevards, skyscrapers and luxury hotels – a bustling, hustling business centre. The new twin tower World Trade Centre is 28 floors high with a west and east tower. On the outskirts, shanty towns or *bidonvilles* present the opposite side of the equation.

Soaring over Casablanca's tower blocks is Morocco's major landmark, and one of the wonders of modern architecture – the *Mosquée Hassan II* (Hassan II Mosque). Opened in August 1993, this graceful building on the shores of the Atlantic has finally given Casablanca a symbolic heart. Plans are underway to remodel much of the city, with a metro and tram system projected along with new avenues leading to the mosque's eight gateways.

To the south, the beach resort of Aïn-Diab is Casa's playground: the perfect antidote to the big city.
Casablanca Tourist Office: 55 rue Omar Slaoui. Tel: (022) 27 11 77.

Aïn-Diab and Marabout de Sidi Abd-er-Rahmane

A corniche road leads to the Aïn-Diab beach clubs, bars and high-class fish restaurants much loved by locals. The clubs all bear exotic names – Tahiti, Lido, Miami – and comprise swimming pools, parasols and restaurants, serenaded by the constant rush of Atlantic rollers. Further on, the long beach of Sidi Abd-er-Rahmane draws enthusiastic soccer players. The marabout after which it is named lies at the far end, a mystical tomb on a small island offshore, accessible only at low tide. Sunsets from here are generally very impressive.
3km (2 miles) south along the Corniche. Bus 9 from boulevard de Paris.

Ancienne Medina (Old Medina)

The Portuguese first settled on this coast in the 15th century. When they returned in the 16th century they named their port Casa Blanca – the white house. This settlement, on a small hill above the bay, was destroyed by the tsunami resulting from the Lisbon earthquake of 1755, and it was not until Arab merchants began to settle in the 19th century that its ruins were cleared and a medina built. Today the medina is sparsely populated and offers little in the way of traditional crafts, although it is a pleasant place to wander.

Anfa

This plush residential district to the west of the centre was once an ancient Phoenician port. It entered modern political history in 1943 when Winston Churchill and President Roosevelt met at the now defunct Anfa Hotel to plan the Allied invasion of Sicily and the 1944 D-Day landings.

Habbous

When Casablanca became the French administrative capital in 1912, thousands of Moroccans moved to the city expecting work. In response to the housing shortage created by these immigrants a new medina, Habbous, was built in the 1930s, mimicking traditional Moroccan architecture. It is a European take on the ideal medina.

Habbous is a spacious district, an enjoyable place to stroll past shops

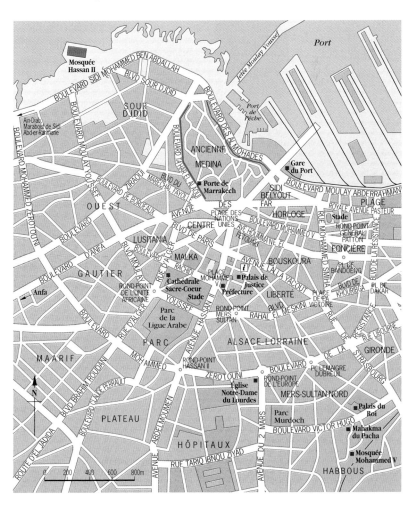

The marble tower of the Hassan II Mosque

the Palais du Roi (Royal Palace). *Boulevard Victor Hugo. Access by bus 5 from boulevard de Paris, or petit taxi.*

Mosquée Hassan II (Hassan II Mosque)

Rightly proclaimed as a triumph of faith and craftsmanship, King Hassan's vast mosque on the shores of the Atlantic was finally opened in August 1993 after six years of construction and an estimated 50 million hours worked by 25,000 labourers. It is the second-largest mosque in the world, after Mecca, and possesses the tallest minaret (200m/656ft high). The mosque's setting, its breathtaking coastal site with Atlantic breakers crashing at its base, was apparently inspired by the Koranic verse: 'the throne of God being on the water'.

The mosque's statistics are impressive: 65,000 tonnes of marble were used, 2,500 columns were erected, and 50 Venetian chandeliers were transported from Italy. A laser beam installed in the minaret is visible 50km (31 miles) away. The prayer hall can accommodate 100,000 worshippers – the size of a small airport terminal. And the whole thing cost some £400 million, raised almost entirely by public donation. All Moroccans contributed (sometimes not voluntarily) and received certificates, many of which are displayed in homes and shops.

Built in white marble, capped with green tiles, the mosque seems a ghostly apparition when viewed from afar, floating above the city. Up close the

selling everything from slippers to olives. The buildings, especially the monumental law courts with their emerald roof and massive towers, suggest a hollow film set. Yet for all its artifice, this is perhaps the least frenetic and most easy-going of Morocco's medinas. To the north are the walls of

craftsmanship of the carvings, colourful tiles and cedar roofing is miraculous: many craft traditions, dormant for centuries, were revived during its construction. In the vast hammam baths an ancient plastering technique called *tadelakt* was used, mixing black soap, egg yolks and plaster, to prevent humidity. Yet modern science complements tradition: the mosque's roof, covering the huge prayer hall is electronic – on sunny days the faithful pray in the open air; when it rains the roof closes.

Boulevard Sidi Mohammed Ben Abdallah. Access by petit taxi. Open to non-Muslims for guided tours only, Sat–Thur 9am, 10am and 11am. Tours last for 1 hour. Admission charge.

Parc de la Ligue Arabe (Arab League Garden)

Rows of palm trees line this shady park in the centre of the city – a place to sit, sip tea in one of the cafés and admire the rose bushes. At the northern end of the park soar the graceful towers of the Cathédrale Sacre-Coeur, once the French cathedral, now closed to the public. Its east wing houses a small medical centre. *South of place Mohammed V.*

Place des Nations Unies (former place Mohammed V)

All major roads to and from Casablanca converge at the hectic place des Nations Unies, just south of the port. The square was renamed in the 1990s, swapping titles with the main administrative square to the southeast.

Here are big hotels, a colonial clock tower, and the constant noise of honking horns and colourful insults.

Place Mohammed V (former place des Nations Unies)

This was the colonial core of Casablanca, built by the French in 1920 to house their main administrative buildings. The style they chose was copied throughout Morocco – 'Mauresque', a blend of Art Deco and Moorish architecture. On the east side of avenue Hassan II are the gilded columns of the Law Courts, the French Consulate and the Préfecture, with its European clock tower. Opposite, the grandiose Post Office looks out on to a wide esplanade dominated by Casablanca's musical fountain, which, if you are lucky, will sing to you and flash lights at night, terrifying the pigeons that inhabit the square.

STREET CONFUSION

Navigating the cities of Morocco is fun and you are guaranteed to get lost. Narrow streets and confusing signage is the norm. The locals also have the propensity to change the name of a street at a whim, and are changing all the names to a muddled Anglo-Arabic format. Sometimes the signage is in French and Arabic, sometimes in the Anglicised Arabic and sometimes just in Arabic script. A street can be a *rue* or a *zankar*. An avenue or boulevard can be a *charih* and a square can be a *place* or *socco*.

Confused? – well, if you aren't, then they do what they did in Casa. They swapped the names of place Mohammed V and place des Nations Unies around!

The medina

Medina simply means 'city', named after the town to which Muhammad fled from Mecca in 622. The medina of Fès is considered to be the most spectacular in the Arab world, a masterpiece of narrow streets and blind alleys enclosed by thick city walls. These maze-like conglomerations provide some of the most memorable sights in Morocco and a chance to witness an ancient way of life at close hand.

The typical medina is made up of several *derbs*, or districts. Traditionally, families of every economic level lived together, the wealthy and notable assuming leadership of the *derb*. These village-like communities were often proudly independent, rather like the various boroughs of New York or London.

While the complexity of the medina is baffling to outsiders, locals have little difficulty negotiating the chaotic streets. In many places only people born and raised in the medina can become policemen, postmen or guides within the walls. Yet the complexity is not without reason: the narrow streets and tall houses ensure privacy and shelter from the elements. Behind their heavy doors, medina houses are quiet and spacious, organised like mosques around central courtyards and fountains.

Each *derb* in the medina contains five requisite facilities, providing for all

The life of Moroccan medinas has changed little in 1,000 years

Traditionally, the medina was protected by high city walls

the daily needs of its inhabitants –
a mosque, a hammam (public bath),
a bakery, a Koranic school and a
fountain. Even today you will see
children carrying flat bread, or *khobza*,
to be baked in the local baker's oven
– the oven also heats water for the
local hammam.

Times are changing for the medinas
of Morocco. The wealthy and notable
have long since moved to plush
residences in the new suburbs. In
their place a wave of immigrants has
arrived from the countryside,
transforming *derb* communities. Many
medinas are in a state of dilapidation,
with traditional lifestyles disappearing
along with historic buildings. One of
the biggest recent threats to medina
life is the purchase of property by
foreigners. The survival of these
unique districts is to a large extent
dependent on tourism. Do not be
daunted – pass through the gateway
and help to preserve the heritage of
Morocco's medieval past.

FÈS

Ancient capital of the Moorish empire, Fès is the intellectual heart of Morocco and one of its oldest cities, established by Moulay Idris I in 789 and developed by Idris II from 809. The world's oldest university lies at its core – the Karaouiyne – still considered one of the greatest Islamic schools in the Arab world. Fassis (as inhabitants are known) have always been at the centre of Morocco's cultural and political life, spreading the reputation of their beloved city throughout North Africa and beyond.

It is a city hidden behind a veil and in a short visit you never penetrate into the soul of Fès – the French called it 'la Mysterieuse'. Fès is Morocco's green city and symbolically the heart of Moroccan Islam (green is the holiest colour).

Fès seems to have had a direct influence on every period in Moroccan history and it was here that the independence movement first took root. Even today it provides a living poll of public opinion in Morocco. Even though it seems in the Ville Nouvelle that many young Moroccans display affluence and embrace Western dress and customs, this is in the main an orthodox, conservative city and has high levels of poverty. Here more than anywhere else in the Arab world does the culture of the materialist West clash with Islamic tradition. Fès remains relatively peaceful, but it does occasionally erupt. In December 1990, disaffected students and a frustrated section of the unemployed rioted and burnt down the Hotel Merenides. No tourists were targeted, but it is wise to steer clear if you spot any demos during your stay.

Divided into three towns, Fès-el-Bali ('the Old Town', founded by Idris I), Fès-el-Jdid ('the New Town', founded by the Merenids in 1276) and the French-built Ville Nouvelle, the city itself is a unique historical monument. Its medina is a medieval maze – passing through its gateways, you are a tolerated alien in a chaotic world that has changed little in over 500 years.

Realising the unique character of Fès, UNESCO began restoring many of its treasures in 1980. Today, the city is attempting to preserve its ancient identity and survive well into the next century.

Fès-el-Bali

Sprawling in the valley, a great sea of houses punctuated by minarets, this is the oldest part of the city, made up of two distinct settlements: the eastern Andalous district, founded by Shiite refugees from Andalucía in 814, and the western Karaouiyne district, founded in 825 by Shiite refugees from Tunisian Kairouan. The Andalousians are said to be the best craftsmen, and to have the most beautiful women. The Karaouiynes are the businessmen. The two districts are very different: Andalous is calmer, Karaouiyne more bustling. Over 250,000 people live in Morocco's largest medina, nicknamed 'the most complicated square mile on earth'.

Fès-el-Jdid

'Fès the New' was built by the Merenids in 1276 as a fortress to guard against rebellious Fassis in the Old Town. Dominated by the Palais Royal, the town became redundant after the French moved the capital to Rabat. Today it has a barren feel, enhanced by the empty houses of the Jewish quarter. Most of the city's 17,000 Jews left for Israel following the 1967 Arab–Israeli War.

Bab Boujeloud

The brightly decorated Bab Boujeloud (*see p64*) is the main entrance to the medina, the traditional gateway to Fès. Its adjacent square has been restructured, with buses and taxis moved to a new station outside the walls.

Bab Dekakène

More a castle than a gateway, the 14th-century 'Gate of the Benches', where criminals were once judged, is an impressive entrance into Fès-el-Jdid. Here, in 1437, a Portuguese prince was hung upside down for four days before being stuffed and displayed by the gate for 30 years. Further on, at Bab Seba, workmen still await potential employers, leaning against the wall, tools in hand, as they have for centuries. *Near western end of avenue des Français.*

Borj Nord

Situated on the northern hillside, Borj Nord is a formidable fortress. It was built in the 16th century by Saadian sultan El Mansour to subdue the Fassis, and offers a panoramic view across the valley; it now houses an arms museum with a 12-tonne cannon called Fatima, used by El Mansour to blow up the Portuguese at the Battle of the Three Kings in 1578.
By the Hotel Merinides. Access by petit taxi. Open: Tue–Sun 8.30am–noon and 2.30–6pm. Admission charge.

Fondouks and souks

Fès is the capital of handicrafts. Its souks offer the finest, although not necessarily the cheapest, Moroccan crafts, and a wander through the teeming streets is unforgettable. Yet this is not a mere tourist attraction: the medina's souks have been here for centuries, a living history that defies the outside world.

The blue exterior of Bab Boujeloud, the main entrance to the Fès medina

Fontaine Nejjarine

Place Nejjarine lies at the end of the Nejjarine (carpenters') souk, a street filled with the scent of cedarwood. The 18th-century fountain in the square is capped by a finely carved canopy, inlaid with colourful mosaics. At the back of the square, the quarter's fondouk (a traditional inn offering accommodation for travellers) is now the Musée Nejjarine (*open: daily 10am–5pm; admission charge*).
20m (22yd) south of Souk Attarine, 20m (22yd) west of Zaouia Moulay Idris II.

Jardins Boujeloud

Escape from the city bustle in these tranquil gardens. A large waterwheel, once used to irrigate the bamboo and exotic flowers, stands to the south. Enjoy a mint tea at the Waterwheel Café.
South of avenue des Français.

Médersa Attarine

Fès is famous for its médersa, dormitory colleges developed by the Merenid dynasty in the 14th century. Each one housed up to 60 students around a central prayer hall, where classes were held. These colleges were phased out after the Middle Ages in the rest of the Islamic world, but survived in Fès until the 1960s. The Médersa

---

MÉDERSA OPENING TIMES

All the médersa in Fès have similar opening times: daily, except Friday morning, 8.30am–5pm. Admission charge (there is no single ticket covering all médersa).

Attarine is one of the finest, built in 1325 – a masterpiece of intricate calligraphy, mosaics and cedar carving. Its arches and pillars seem weightless, supporting galleries of monastic-like cells where students lived. It is closed for restoration until 2010.
East of Souk Attarine, opposite the Karaouiyne Mosque.

Médersa Bou Inania

The Médersa Bou Inania is the most beautiful of all Merenid monuments. Built on an even more impressive scale than the Attarine, not a centimetre of its façades is left unadorned. It was built by Abou Inan, a sultan famous for committing gruesome murders and fathering 325 sons. Legend states that he was criticised by religious elders for marrying a prostitute in 1355. He proceeded to build the Médersa Bou Inania on a garbage dump and invited the elders to admire it. When they expressed amazement at its beauty he replied: 'As from garbage comes beauty, so now my wife has become pure.'

Outside, the famous water clock was also installed by Abou Inan (who wished to have the time of prayer called from his médersa rather than the Karaouiyne). A recently discovered parchment has revealed how it worked.
100m (110yd) from Bab Boujeloud on rue Talaa Kebira.

Médersa Cherratine

This is the largest and youngest college in Fès, with a capacity for 240 students.

Built under the Alaouites in 1670, its style is much more utilitarian than that of the older médersa. Student rooms are constructed around three courtyards, with latrines and washbasins around the fourth courtyard. There are 120 rooms in total. The médersa was inhabited as recently as 1950 by theology students from the Karaouiyne mosque.
Southwest corner of the Karaouiyne.

Médersa Seffarine

Médersa Seffarine is the oldest médersa in Fès, founded in 1280 and hiding away down a small lane from place Seffarine. Through the studded door, the interior resembles a traditional house, its arched balcony suggesting intimate family life rather than spiritual retreat.
Place Seffarine.

Médersa Sehrij

Isolated in the Andalous district, the Sehrij predates its more illustrious cousins in the Karaouiyne quarter, having been built in 1321. It retains a peaceful and strangely bewitching atmosphere – the main attraction here is a small ablutions pool filled with water, which reflects the crumbling carvings.
20m (22yd) south of Andalous Mosque.

Mellah

Each Moroccan city has a *mellah*, or Jewish quarter, witness to Morocco's history of cultural diversity. The Fassi *Mellah* was the original; the word means 'salt', a reference to the practice of salting

the severed heads of enemies – a task given to the Jews. Now empty, the *Mellah* still retains a veneer of decaying opulence. The Hebrew cemetery, beautifully restored by UNESCO, is a poignant reminder of the past.
South of rue Bou Ksissat. The cemetery is open daily 8.30am–6pm.
Admission free.

Mosquée des Andalous (Andalous Mosque)

The heart of the Andalous district is dominated by this majestic mosque, constructed in 860 by Miriam, the sister
(*Cont. on p62*)

Ritual purification at Médersa Bou Inania

Islamic architecture

Since AD 622, when Muhammad founded the first mosque in Medina, Islamic building has been intimately linked with the Koran, the direct word of God. The mosque (literally 'place of prostration') is oriented towards Mecca, Muhammad's birthplace. This direction is marked by the *mihrab*, a small prayer niche where the *imam*, or spiritual leader, will stand to lead prayer. Hung from the ceiling are candelabra, symbolising Allah, who is the light of the universe. The mosque forecourt, the *sahn*, contains a pool or fountain for ritual ablutions decreed in the Koran. Above the mosque is a minaret, where the call to prayer (*adhan*) is issued five times a day. Moroccan minarets are distinctively square, in contrast to cylindrical versions further east.

The great Almohad tower of the Koutoubia in Marrakech created a style that was adopted throughout Morocco; the new Hassan II minaret in Casablanca is a direct descendant.

Although Islam forbids iconography, it rejoices in decoration. While Moroccan mosques are usually unadorned, the médersa of Fès, Meknès and Marrakech are intricately ornate. *Zellij* mosaic decorations, delicate calligraphy or 'God's spiders' webs' cover façades and columns. Such art seeks to draw attention from the real world towards a more spiritual one. The repetition of patterns, seemingly endless, seeks not to focus the eye but to liberate it, to take it towards paradise. Black and white interlocking patterns often surround the médersa, symbolising the opposite forces of good and evil, while below them a single verse from the Koran is repeated in angular Kufic calligraphy – 'God is great. There is no God but God...'

Islamic architecture is characterised by its subtle dimensions and intricate calligraphy

The keyhole arches and gateways found everywhere in Morocco are also influenced by the Koran. Straight doorways are crowned by an arch representing paradise: Muslims believe that heaven is guarded by seven gateways, through which the faithful must pass.

Three of the seven gateways to the Palais Royal in Fès, with their characteristic Islamic horseshoe arches

The Karaouiyne Mosque and courtyard – the mosque has been altered by every ruler since its foundation

of Fatima, who built the Karaouiyne. The mosque was also used as a university with scholars housed in the neighbouring Sebbayin and Sehrij médersa (*see p59*).

Mosquée Karaouiyne

All streets in the medina are said to lead to the Karaouiyne, its spiritual centre. The mosque was founded in 859 by Fatima el Fihri in memory of her Tunisian father, and became the greatest university of the medieval Arab world. In the 10th century Pope Sylvester II studied here, before introducing Arabic mathematics to Europe. Classes are still held in the mosque, but it is above all a religious centre. Non-Muslims are not permitted access.
East of Souk Attarine.

Palais Dar Batha (Musée Dar Batha)

Dar Batha palace was built in 1873 by Hassan I in a bid to unify the towns of Fès. His reign was short and the palace was subsequently used by his son Abd el Aziz, the 'playboy of Fès', for wild parties. Under the Protectorate, the building became a fine crafts museum.

Eight rooms are ranged around a central courtyard. Visitors must take a guided tour, but do not be hurried. Begin with the pottery room, full of local ceramics from the 13th century using the blue of Fès, extracted from cornflowers. Fès is also famous for its double-sided embroidery.

A further room is dominated by colossal Berber rugs, and cases of sturdy Berber jewellery from the Middle Atlas. Ornate doorways and gigantic locks used to close the medina at night are exhibited next door, including a 1,100-year-old inscription from the Karaouiyne Mosque, and a magnificent 16th-century marble doorway from the El Badi Palace in Marrakech.

The pretty Andalusian garden hosts concerts in the summer.
Boujeloud/place de l'Istiqlal, south of Bab Boujeloud. Tel: (035) 63 41 16. Open: daily 8am–4.30pm. Admission charge.

Palais Royal (Dar el Makhzen)

This vast palace complex is the biggest in Morocco, extended over seven centuries by various Moroccan sultans but unfortunately, like all the royal palaces, closed to visitors. An idea of its extravagant decoration is given by the gateways on place des Alaouites. These seven brass doors, delicately engraved by Fès' finest craftsmen, were commissioned by Hassan II in 1968, and represent the seven gateways to the heavens of Islam. The surrounding mosaics symbolise the union of the blue of Fès with the green of the Prophet, while the inscription above the gateways reads 'Welcome. Enter in Peace.' Twice a year the brass is meticulously cleaned. *Place des Alaouites.*

Place Seffarine

This picturesque square is home to the copperworkers of Fès, who hammer at huge couscous pots alongside the ancient fig trees. The fountain in the wall of the Karaouiyne library (one of the most important in the Islamic world, but closed to visitors) was made by a Portuguese slave in the 18th century: locals were so impressed that he was freed.
Southeast corner of the Karaouiyne Mosque.

Quartier Moulay Abdallah

The area around the town's two main mosques is quiet and somewhat reserved. Under the Protectorate this was divided from the rest of the town, with bars, restaurants and brothels set up for French soldiers.

Tombeaux Mérinides

Perched on the northern hillside, these crumbling ruins are all that remain of an extensive necropolis, built to house the Merenid sultans. From this ghostly setting the view over the valley is superb – a seething mass of houses and fragile minarets (there are said to be 365 mosques in the medina alone). *Next to the Hotel Merinides.*

Ville Nouvelle

The new town comprises the main administrative buildings along avenue Hassan II and the hub of café society and shops on boulevard Mohammed V. It is the best place to go for coffee.

Zaouia Moulay Idris II (Mausoleum of Moulay Idris II)

The shrine of the developer of Fès was forbidden to non-Muslims until the French occupation in 1911. Today visitors can walk under the wooden bar designed to keep out animals and infidels (it is unwise to photograph the interior – this is the second most holy site in Morocco). Its lavish decoration, including clocks and silverware donated by pilgrims, is matched by the dedicated attention of worshippers who come seeking *baraka*, or a blessing. *West of the Karaouiyne. Closed to non-Muslims.*

FAUX GUIDES

During your stay in Morocco you will encounter unofficial, '*faux*' or 'false' guides. They may show you one sight, and then want to take you to a carpet shop where doubtless they'll gain a commission on your purchases if you are foolish enough to make any. Don't be fooled by them, and ignore their taunts if they become abusive. Authorities have clamped down on *faux* guides so they are not so numerous now, and far less aggressive.

Walk: Fès Old Town

This walk takes you into the heart of the medina, a journey back in time through the most colourful souks in Morocco. Begin first thing in the morning.

Allow 4 hours. It is advisable to hire a guide from your hotel or riad, if only to fend off other 'helpers'.

Begin at Bab Boujeloud.

1 Bab Boujeloud

Built in 1913, this main gateway remains resolutely traditional – a foretaste of the medina itself. Blue-tiled on the outside (the colour of Fès) and green on the inside (the colour of Islam), its archway frames the bustle of the main street, enticing the uninitiated.

Head straight along rue Talaa Kebira, the main thoroughfare; 80m (90yd) on your right is Médersa Bou Inania.

2 Médersa Bou Inania

The greatest of Fès' médersa, Bou Inania is the only active religious building in the city that is open to non-Muslims (*see p58*).

Continue downhill to Souk Attarine, and the spice stalls and jewellers. Just after the Dar Saada restaurant, turn right.

3 Zaouia Moulay Idris II

Five centuries after Moulay Idris' death, a perfectly preserved body was found on this spot in the centre of Fès'

medina. Since then, worshippers have flocked to the site, thronging the ornately decorated *zaouia* (shrine). The saint is now patron to many causes, including childless women and nougat vendors, whose stalls surround his mausoleum (*see p63*).

Head east through the Kissaria fabric souk to the Karaouiyne Mosque.

4 Mosquée Karaouiyne

When Fatima el Fihri decided to build a mosque in 859 to honour her dead father, she consulted the wisest men of the day as to its location. Once it was chosen, she used only materials dug from this site, to ensure the mosque's purity. Consequently, this is the holiest ground in Morocco (*see p62*).

Walking round the north side of the mosque, you will see Médersa Attarine on your left.

5 Médersa Attarine

This is the second most beautiful of the Fès médersa and probably one of the

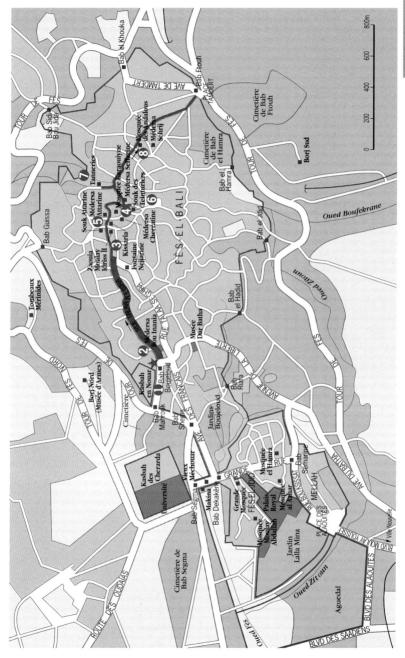

The dark green tiles of the Mosquée Karaouiyne in the foreground are the symbolic colour of Islam

oldest. It was founded by the Merenid sultan Abou Said in 1325. The Zellij pattern is extraordinarily complex, with interlaced pentagons and stars. Lower down it seems as if a new craftsman was employed as the pattern changes in formation. It is closed for restoration until 2010.

Walk south to place Seffarine and take the small left-hand street at the end of the square. This leads to the dyers' souk.

6 Souk des Teinturiers

Dyers have inhabited and worked in this small street, also called Souk Sabbighin, since the 10th century. Even today the blackened workshops where pots bubble and fires roar seem to exist in another age. Traditionally the dyes were always natural vegetable colouring, but nowadays chemicals are frequently used.

Head back to place Seffarine. Take rue Méchatine north – a well-trodden path despite its narrowness.

7 Tanneries

The tanneries of Souk Dabbaghin are a mesmerising sight – workers dressed only in shorts leap among huge vats, plunging skins into mixtures of dye and pigeon droppings (used to soften the leather). Skins are left for up to two weeks to colour, then dried on the hillsides, as they have since the 16th century. It could be euphemistically called a 'place with odour'.

Return southwards to cross Oued Fès at Pont Bein el Moudoun into the Andalous quarter. Rue Seffrah then rises to the Andalous Mosque.

8 Mosquée des Andalous (Andalous Mosque)

Sister to the Karaouiyne, the Andalous Mosque is famous for its huge carved doorway, built by the Almohads. It is from here, at the highest point of the medina, that the end of Ramadan is announced.

Continue down rue Fekharine to Bab Ftouh. Take a taxi from here back to your hotel.

Walk: Fès Old Town

Hives of activity in the midst of the tanneries

Central plains, Moyen Atlas and the Atlantic coast

MEKNÈS

When the Berber Meknassas tribe settled in this fertile valley in the 10th century, they founded a city that was to become the capital of an empire. For 700 years Meknès rested in relative obscurity – a trading post fought over for its rich farmland. In 1672, Moulay Ismaïl, one of Morocco's most powerful sultans, chose Meknès as his home. He proceeded to build a colossal town to rival the court of his contemporary Louis XIV of France at Versailles.

Little has happened in Meknès since then. After a brief fling with notoriety during French occupation, Meknès still retains the air of a provincial farming town, albeit one boasting some of the most extravagant sights in Morocco.

Meknès Tourist Office: place Administrative. Tel: (035) 51 60 22.

Bab Mansour

Proclaimed as the greatest gateway in North Africa, Bab Mansour is the symbol of Moulay Ismaïl's magnificent architectural vision. It is named after its architect, a Christian slave who converted to Islam. Legend has it that on its completion El Mansour was asked by the sultan if he could do even better. Yes, he replied, and was promptly executed. The gate was actually finished by Ismaïl's son Moulay Abdullah, whose praises are sung in the inscription around the top. Its monumental style is enhanced by two flanking arcades, supported by

Bab Mansour, the finest gateway in North Africa

marble pillars ransacked from Roman Volubilis (*see p77*).
Place el Hedim.

Bassin de l'Agdal (Agdal Basin)

This vast pool – 400m (1,312ft) long, 100m (328ft) wide and 4m (13ft) deep, fed by 24km (15 miles) of canals from the Middle Atlas – was built by Moulay Ismaïl to provide water for his troops in time of siege. It was enjoyed by his wives (reputedly numbering an amazing 500), who would stroll along its banks. Today it is popular with joggers, who circle it.
South of Dar el Makhzen, next to Heri as Souani.

Dar Kebira

Dar Kebira, or Imperial City, contained 50 palaces in its 17th-century heyday. At its opening ceremony in 1677, Moulay Ismaïl ritually severed the head of a wolf and stuck it on the gate as a symbol of his power. This entrance on the left past Moulay Ismaïl's mausoleum leads to the ruined complex – there is little to see: a few massive blocks of stone, only hinting at the extravagance of the past. Opposite is the **Dar el Makhzen**, still a royal residence whose gardens, once playground to the sultan's harem, are now a royal golf course. From here, 25km (16 miles) of dramatic red walls surround the city, an ample illustration of Moulay Ismaïl's lust for building. These provide a spectacular backdrop for Meknès' annual autumn Fantasia,

MOULAY ISMAÏL (*c.*1634–1727)

Moulay Ismaïl is a legendary figure in Morocco. He united the country's warring tribes, defended the kingdom against Turkish invasion, and chased the English and Spanish from the northern coast. Yet he is remembered as much for his spectacular cruelty as for his impressive political achievements.

His first act as sultan was to dispatch 700 enemy heads to Fès and Marrakech – a warning to prospective rebels. He had 30,000 slaves building Meknès; it was said he would slice off their heads at will and build bridges from the lashed bodies of prisoners.

He had 500 sons and countless daughters (many were strangled at birth), and attempted to marry the daughter of the French king Louis XIV (he was refused). He was protected by a fearsome bodyguard of 25,000 Sudanese slaves, whose descendants guard the present king.

That Moulay Ismaïl is still revered in Morocco may seem surprising. But he was, by all accounts, a deeply religious man. He tried to convert the English king James II to Islam. His explanation for his tyrannical behaviour was simple: 'My subjects are rats in a sack. If I do not keep shaking the sack they will bite their way through.'

a huge celebration when Berber horsemen simulate past battles, firing muskets with great glee.
Northeast of place Lalla Aouda.
Open access. Admission free.

Heri as Souanl (Royal Granary)

From the royal palace and the vast square where foreign ambassadors were received, you come to the royal granary. These cavernous storage rooms are remarkably cool in summer – 4m (13ft) thick walls ensure that the temperature is constantly below 18°C (64°F). Grain was poured in from the high windows and ground by huge millstones turned by three horses. Deep wells provided water directly from the neighbouring Agdal basin. Look out for the 'sun door', taken from the royal palace: its decorations resemble an expanding sun, supposedly inspired by the French 'Sun King', Louis XIV. The elegant arches at the back of the granaries are remains of further storerooms, whose roof collapsed during the 1755 Lisbon earthquake.

The Médersa Bou Inania

These are often described by local guides as the Sultan's Stables; given that he kept 12,000 horses, this seems a tenuous claim. The real stables are 2km (1¹/₄ miles) further on, and closed to visitors.

South of the royal palace, next to the Agdal Basin. Open: daily 9am–noon & 3–6.30pm. Admission charge.

Koubbet el Khiaytin (Prison of Christian Slaves)

This immense underground vault was reputed to be the prison for Moulay Ismaïl's 2,500 Christian slaves, captured by the 'Sallee Rovers' pirates of Rabat (*see p80*). It is said that many slaves refused to leave the safety of their dark refuge – during construction of the Imperial City most of them died where they toiled, and their bodies were mixed into the cement of the walls. Wild myths about the chambers have always kept Meknès' tourist guides in business. One states that three tunnels lead from the chamber to Rabat, Fès and Volubilis. A French tourist did, in fact, disappear down here in 1951, and the tunnels were subsequently blocked up. Scholars now believe the subterranean vaults were nothing more than storerooms for armaments.

Above ground, the small domed building was used by Moulay Ismaïl to receive foreign dignitaries.

Place Lalla Aouda. Open: daily 9am–noon & 3–6pm. Admission charge.

The Royal Granary once held supplies to feed an army of 50,000 soldiers

Médersa Bou Inania

Many believe this small médersa to be the finest in Morocco, surpassing even its namesake in Fès. It was founded by Abou el Hassan, builder of the Chellah in Rabat, and finished by his son, Abou Inan. Through a narrow hallway opposite the medina's main mosque, the small courtyard, or *sahn*, is a sanctuary from the animation of the streets, its stucco walls adorned with calligraphy. Stairs lead up to a gallery of 13 rooms, occupied by students as recently as 1964 – two students shared a room, reading Koranic scriptures by candlelight. From here steps lead to the roof, providing a rare view of the huddle of the medina, across the emerald roofs of the mosque. *Souk es Sebat. Open: daily 9am–noon & 3–6.30pm. Admission charge.*

Medina

The medina of Meknès, while not as frenetic nor as ancient as that in Fès,

Intricate cedar and stucco carving from the Médersa Bou Inania

a series of chaotic souks, metalworkers and carpenters, all vying for trade. Continue northwest through Bab el Jdid, outside the walls, to the green-roofed Koubba de Sidi Aïssa (Marabout of Ben Aïssa). Worshippers of this saint, the Aissaoua, are the most fanatical in Morocco. While in trances they are said to pierce themselves with knives, eat live snakes and scorpions and bite heads off chickens. The marabout is closed to non-Muslims and it is unwise to approach too closely.

Musée Dar Jamaï (Dar Jamaï Museum)

Built by the same family of viziers (chancellors) as the Palais Jamaï in Fès, this 19th-century palace is now one of Morocco's finest museums, set in galleries surrounding a pretty Andalusian garden. On the ground floor are displays of ceramics and jewellery, as well as stunning carpets from the Middle Atlas. Upstairs is a reconstruction of the vizier's reception room with an immaculate decorative cedar ceiling. Note also the magnificent silk curtain separating the bedroom on the right. The embroidered cushions are a speciality of Meknès.

Place el Hédim. Open: 9am–5pm. Closed: Tue. Admission charge.

Tombeau de Moulay Ismaïl (Moulay Ismaïl Tomb)

The last resting place of the flamboyant Moulay Ismaïl is surprisingly subdued. The shrine is open to non-Muslims, but

has few tourists and offers a rare glimpse of medina life as it has been led for over a thousand years. It is easy to negotiate and fairly hassle-free. The centre of the medina is dominated by upmarket goods – slippers, Western shoes and kaftans. West of here, following the street from the mosque, is Souk Nejjarine, the carpenters' souk. Just to the left is Souk Joutiya as-Zerabi, by a small mosque, where Berber carpets are sold. To the north is

visitors should dress respectfully. Several antechambers lead to the main courtyard, where you are required to remove your shoes. Inside, the mausoleum is intricately sculpted, in contrast to Moulay Ismaïl's own epic style. There are four tombs: Moulay Ismaïl lies second from the left, next to his wife and two sons. Behind them stand two grandfather clocks, commiseration presents from the French king Louis XIV in 1700, after he refused Moulay Ismaïl's marital advances towards his daughter. The extensive marble surrounds came from Carrara, in Italy. Salt was bartered in return – 1kg (2¼lb) of salt for 1kg (2¼lb) of marble.

South of place Lalla Aouda, through Bab Moulay Ismaïl. Open: 9am–noon & 3–6.30pm. Closed: Fri morning. Admission free.

An austere façade hides the tomb of the flamboyant Sultan Moulay Ismaïl

Walk: Meknès Old Town

A walk from the medieval medina to the Imperial City of Moulay Ismaïl.

Allow 3 hours. Avoid noon–3pm, when the monuments are closed.

Begin at the medina gateway on rue Aqbet Ezziadine. Through the arch, turn right on to rue Rabah Kedima Karmouni to the kissaria. Go under another arch, turn left, noting the textile boutiques, passing Kissama el Harir on the left, and continue for 50m (55yd) to the mosque. Follow the walls right and then left on to the medina's main street, Souk es Sebbat. Here are stalls selling fresh mint – Meknès mint is claimed to be the best in Morocco. Another 20m (22yd) on is the Médersa Bou Inania.

1 Médersa Bou Inania

A masterpiece of Merenid art, the 'Jewel of the Medina' is impressive for its subtlety. To the right of the ablutions pool is a small prayer hall and *mihrab* facing Mecca, and surrounding the courtyard are immaculately preserved cedarwood screens, or *moucharabieh* (literally 'see without being seen'), which allowed students a certain privacy. Such screens were also an integral part of harems, behind which wives would languish. The médersa has been fully restored.

Take the road opposite the médersa and turn right at the fountain. Follow the road round to the left and then turn right and head into place el Hédim.

2 Place el Hédim

'The square of destruction' is rumoured to be where Moulay Ismaïl carried out many executions or may be named after the houses destroyed to clear a road to his palace. Remodelled in 1980, it has little of its former charm. Cafés on the right provide welcome shade and drinks.

Across the plaza is the entrance to the Imperial City, Bab Mansour.

3 Bab Mansour

This monumental gateway escapes few cameras.

Continue to place Lalla Aouda.

4 Place Lalla Aouda

This recently renovated square is named after one of Moulay Ismaïl's

favourite daughters. It is said she succumbed to eating a peach during Ramadan, and to atone for her sins built a médersa. To the left are shops selling wool. To the right is the Koubbet el Khiaytin (*see p70*) on a remodelled square.
Head through Bab Moulay Ismaïl.

5 Tombeau de Moulay Ismaïl (Mausoleum of Moulay Ismaïl)

The tomb of the tyrannical and much respected sultan is on the left, just through the ornamental gateway. Beyond the entrance hall lie three courtyards, followed by the tomb hall of Moulay Ismaïl and his family (*see pp72–3*).
Walk on from the mausoleum, through Bab el Rih (Gate of the Winds) to the 'Interminable Wall'.

6 Mur Interminable (The Interminable Wall)

The 'interminable wall' or 'wall of death', so called because prisoners marched along it to their execution, stretches for 1km (²/₃ mile) between Dar Kebira on the left and the royal palace on the right.
At the end of the wall turn right and continue past the palace entrance, through the double gates. Heri as Souani is 50m (55yd) ahead.

7 Heri as Souani (Royal Granary)

It is said that 24 pavilions once surmounted the granary, comprising the hidden chambers of the sultan's harem. After your visit to the granary (*see p69*) walk around the Agdal pool.
Take a taxi back into town.

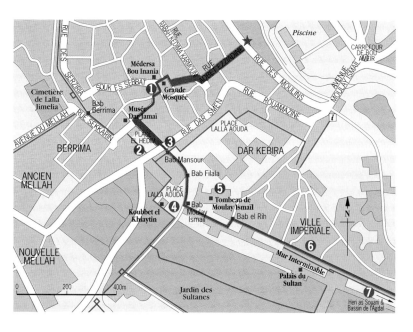

Central plains, Moyen Atlas and the Atlantic coast

Ornamental walls of the royal palace, where Moulay Ismaïl would drive a chariot pulled by eunuchs

MEKNÈS ENVIRONS
Col du Zeggota
An ideal place for a picnic, with views over the fertile Meknès plain.
15km (9 miles) north of Moulay Idris.

Moulay Idris
Morocco's holiest town and resting place of Moulay Idris. Non-Muslims are now allowed in but cannot visit the tomb. Instead, climb to the Sidi Abdallah el Hajjam terrace (a guide is necessary).

From here you can see the green roof of the *zaouia* (tomb) and the courtyard. Below is the unique cylindrical minaret of the town's newest mosque, built in 1939.

Moulay Idris is the site of Morocco's most revered festival, the *moussem*, in late August/early September. A very religious occasion, it is open to discreet visitors.
27km (17 miles) north of Meknès, 47km (29 miles) west of Fès.

MOULAY IDRIS – FOUNDER OF ARABIC MOROCCO

A direct descendant of the Prophet Muhammad, Moulay Idris fled Mecca in 787, following defeat by the Caliph of Baghdad. He landed in Morocco and was welcomed in Volubilis, becoming their *imam* (spiritual and political leader). A charismatic figure, he soon converted the Berber tribes to Islam and moved their town to a better-defended site between two hills. In 792, wary of Moulay Idris' growing power, the Caliph of Baghdad sent an agent to Morocco to poison the great leader. He was buried in the town, while his son went on to expand the city of Fès.

Volubilis

Morocco's most important Roman town lies in the wide Meknès plain beneath the Zerhoun mountains.

There was a settlement here during the Neolithic period, but it was Juba II who put Volubilis on the political map in 25 BC. A descendant of Hannibal, he married Cleopatra's daughter and introduced Roman civilisation. His son, Ptolemy, was murdered by Caligula in AD 40 and Volubilis came under direct Roman control. The Romans remained here until Vandals invaded in AD 285. Settlements came and went, but the town was finally deserted in the 18th century.

Volubilis is famous for its mosaics. One in the House of Orpheus depicts Orpheus charming the animals with his lyre. Nearby, Neptune rides his sea horse, while another mosaic depicts swastika designs – symbols of good luck that originated in India.

Most of the visible ruins date from the 3rd century AD. In the centre of the town stands the basilica and temple of Jupiter. To the north is the Arc de Triomphe, which was reconstructed in 1915 from sketches made by William Boyd in 1726. From here, the Decumanus Maximus, the main street in AD 200, extends northeast. Its houses were the most wealthy in Roman Volubilis – stunning mosaics adorn their floors, from the dark red seafood of the House of Ephebus to the portrayals of Diana and her Nymphs in the House of Venus.

4km (2¹/₂ miles) northwest of Moulay Idris. Open: daily, sunrise to sunset. Admission charge.

Zellij tiles decorate the tomb of Moulay Ismaïl

MOYEN ATLAS (MIDDLE ATLAS)

Giant cedar forests, volcanic mountains, strings of lakes and wind-swept plains grace the Middle Atlas, just 60km (37 miles) south of Fès.

Beni-Mellal

The largest town in the Middle Atlas with a population of 250,000, Beni-Mellal is a pleasant stopover between Fès and Marrakech. The surrounding plains are an immensely fertile area: oranges, olives and sugar cane are produced there.

289km (180 miles) southwest of Fès, 194km (121 miles) northeast of Marrakech.

Khenifra

Khenifra, in the midst of the Middle Atlas plateau, is a large garrison town with few sights, notable for its strange, dark red buildings and isolated location. Its souks are highly traditional – few tourists venture here.

The S303 north to Aïn-Leuh offers a breathtaking drive through deep gorges and into cedar forests where you will see families of Barbary apes (*see p137*).

82km (51 miles) southwest of Azrou, 234km (145 miles) northeast of Marrakech. Souks: Wed & Sun.

Midelt to the Ziz

South on the N13 to Midelt, the scenery begins to change and the hills become more arid. At the base of the massive Jbel Ayachi range is **Midelt** – the

TAZA'S MAGICIAN

One of Taza's most infamous sons, Bou Hamra, travelled the countryside performing 'miracles' in the 19th century. His star turn involved a conversation with a 'corpse', in which a supposedly dead accomplice was buried in a grave. The man was able to breathe and speak through a thin straw and an amazed crowd heard a 'voice from the dead'. Bou Hamra would then crush the straw with his foot and the accomplice would asphyxiate, to be dug up as a real corpse. The magician met his own end in 1908: he was dragged to Fès, offered to the court lions, who refused to eat him, and subsequently shot.

middle of Morocco, famous for its carpets (the most impressive workshop is run by Franciscan nuns – follow signs to Jaffar). West of Midelt is the **Cirque de Jaffar**, a stunning gravel track rising to 3,700m (12,139ft). South of Midelt, just after the inappropriately named village of Rich, you pass through the **Tunnel du Légionnaire**, built by the French Foreign Legion in 1930, and descend into the dramatic **Gorges du Ziz**, a breathtaking canyon of verdant oases.

Midelt 210km (130 miles) south of Fès. Souk: Sun.

Sefrou and Ifrane valleys

South of Fès two main roads run into the Middle Atlas. Of these, the **Ifrane Valley** is the more attractive, rising to Immouzer from where tracks lead east to a necklace of small lakes. Further south is **Ifrane**, an apparition of Alpine-style chalets built by French administrators as a ski centre for nearby Mischliffen. This is now one of Morocco's most bourgeois resorts – the king has a large palace in the hills. From Ifrane to Azrou the road offers dramatic views down into the Jaba Valley. **Azrou** remains a typical Middle Atlas town, and is a centre for local woodcrafts. Walks in the cedar forests can be arranged here.

The alternative route south, along the Sefrou Valley, is more desolate. **Sefrou** is an interesting town, with an ancient, well-stocked medina and ochre walls dating from Moulay Ismaïl's day. Its *mellah* is extensive, although most Jews left in 1967. The town is famous for its cherry festival in June.

Azrou: 60km (37 miles) south of Meknès. Souk: Tue. Sefrou: 28km (17 miles) south of Fès. Souk: Thur.

Taza

The Taza gap is the only natural pass between the Eastern Rif and the rest of Morocco. The Almohads built defensive walls around Taza in 1135, as well as the impressive **Bab el Rih** (Gate of the Winds). Other sights include Bou Hamra's palace (*see box opposite*).

To the south, the **Tazzeka National Park** around Jbel Tazzeka provides spectacular hiking (*see p140*).

Villages hug the slopes of the southern Middle Atlas mountains

Central plains, Moyen Atlas and the Atlantic coast

RABAT

Rabat is a city of many faces: it is an old Roman port, an Almohad staging post for the invasion of Spain (*Ribat el Fath*, or 'camp of victory', the origin of its name), a pirate base and, since 1912, it has been the administrative capital of Morocco.

Although, in part, a Westernised capital, Rabat is proud of its more ancient history: it boasts some of the most impressive imperial monuments in the country. Across the Bou Regreg estuary is Salé, once home to the fearsome 'Sallee Rovers', who were marauding pirates of the 17th century. *Rabat Tourist Office: 23 avenue de la Victoire. Tel: (037) 77 99 69.*

Chellah

Within the Merenid walls of the Chellah are the most hauntingly beautiful ruins in Morocco. Set in a garden of tropical plants are the remains of ancient Roman Sala Colonia and the necropolis of the great Merenid leader El Hassan. The tomb of the mighty 'Black Sultan' lies in a small walled mausoleum, alongside his favourite wife, Shams ed Doura, or 'morning light', an English convert to Islam. Guides will show you round the crumbling halls and point out the slender minaret. To the right of the tombs is a small pool shaded by a banana tree. Here women come to feed eggs to the dark eels that live in its depths – this strange marabout is said to grant fertility.

Boulevard Moussa Ibn Noussair. Open: daily 8.30am–5.30pm. Admission charge.

Kasbah des Oudaïas

Squatting snugly at the mouth of the estuary, the Kasbah des Oudaïas was built by the Almohads in the 12th century. Its main gate, the dramatic Bab Oudaïa, is arguably the finest gate in the Islamic world. The repetitive palm frond motif was designed to inspire contemplation and not to impress. From here, walk along rue Jamaa to the Platforme. Three hundred years ago, the estuary below was filled with pirate ships, which lured schooners on to the sandbanks. Guns from the kasbah would then finish them off. Nearby is a small carpet workshop, where you will be invited to sit with the women weavers (for a tip).

Moulay Ismaïl's former palace is inside the kasbah walls. Now an intriguing Moroccan jewellery museum, it was a former Museum of Moroccan Arts. Moulay Ismaïl greatly favoured Rabat, installing his mercenary guard of Oudaya tribesmen in the kasbah.

The Andalusian gardens of the kasbah are exquisite and perfect: this is a favourite meeting place for local women, among the fragrant chaos of flowers and citrus trees. Through the gateway overlooking Salé and the estuary is the Café Maure, an institution in Rabat for afternoon tea. *Kasbah des Oudaïas. Tel: (037) 73 15 37. Open: 10am–4pm. Closed: Tue. Admission charge.*

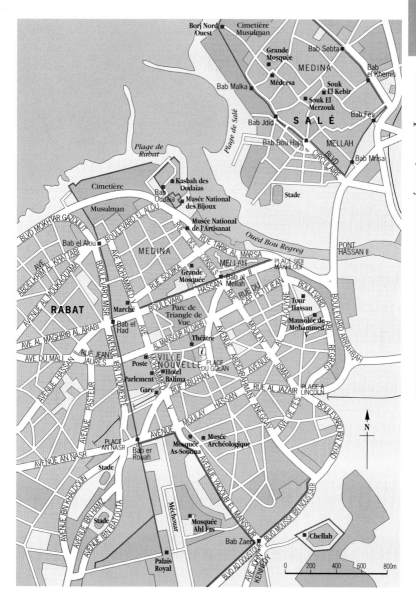

Bord Nord Ouest
Cimetière Musulman
Grande Mosquée
Bab Sebta
MEDINA
Bab el Khemis
Bab Malka
Médersa
Souk El Kebir
Souk El Merzouk
Bab Fès
Bab Jdid
SALÉ
MELLAH
Bab Bou Haja
Bab Mrisa
BLVD CIRCULAIRE
Stade
Plage de Salé

Plage de Rabat
Kasbah des Oudaias
Bab Oudaïa
Musée National des Bijoux
Cimetière
Musée National de l'Artisanat
Musulman
Oued Bou Regreg
PONT HASSAN II
BLVD MOKHTAR GAZOULIT
BOULEVARD EL ALOU
RUE DES CONSULS
RUE TARIK AL MARSA
Bab el Alou
MEDINA
MELLAH
PLACE SIDI MAKHLOUF
AVE ABDELKRIM AL KHATTABI
AVE AL MOUKAOUAMA
AVENUE MOHAMMED V
RUE SOUIKA
Grande Mosquée
Bab al Mellah
BOULEVARD ABI REGREG
BOULEVARD ARRAHBAH
RABAT
BOULEVARD MISR
Marché
BOULEVARD HASSAN II
RUE DU CAP PETITJEAN
Tour Hassan
AVE MAGHRIB AL ARABI
Bab el Had
Parc de Triangle de Vue
AL MANSOUR AD DAHBI
Mausolée de Mohammed
AVENUE MOULAY
AVENUE HASSAN
Théâtre
i
RUE JEAN JAURES
AVE DU MALI
Poste
VILLE NOUVELLE
PLACE DU GOLAN
AVENUE PASTEUR
AVENUE IBN TOUMERTE
Parlement
Hotel Balima
AVENUE ABDERRAHMAN ANEGGAY
AVE DE FES
PLACE A LINCOLN
Gare
RUE ABUHAN
MOULAY HASSAN
RUE AL JAZAIR
BOULEVARD IBN ZIYAD
PLACE AN NASR
AVENUE
Bab er Rouah
Mosquée As-Sounna
Musée Archéologique
AVENUE AN NASR
Stade
AVENUE IBN KHALDOUN
AVENUE IBN HAZM
MOULAY HASSAN
N
Méchouar
Stade
AVENUE IBN BATTOUTA
Mosquée Ahl Fas
AVENUE YACOUB EL MANSOUR
BLVD MOUSSA IBN MOUSSAIR
Chellah
Bab Zaers
Palais Royal
BLVD AD DOUSTOUR
AVE JOHN KENNEDY
0 200 400 600 800m

Shimmering gold decorates the roof above Mohammed V's tomb

Mausolée de Mohammed V and La Tour Hassan

Begun by Yacoub el Mansour in 1195 to celebrate victories in Spain, the Hassan tower is all that remains of the greatest Almohad monument in Morocco. This huge mosque was designed as the biggest in the world, but construction was stopped on the day of El Mansour's death in 1199. The 50m (164ft) high minaret, uncharacteristically placed in the middle of the prayer hall, was originally supposed to soar 80m (262ft); six ramps still lead to its summit, designed to allow the sultan to ride to the top. Each of the four façades is carved with different designs. The 355 re-erected columns at its base once supported an immense roof, destroyed by the Lisbon earthquake of 1755.

Opposite is the white mausoleum of King Hassan's father, Mohammed V, who died in 1961. The dazzling Carrara marble tomb was designed by Vietnamese architect Vo Toan, and its interior, a masterpiece of Moroccan craftsmanship, is a fitting resting place for the man who led Morocco to independence. To the side is a smaller sarcophagus containing King Hassan's brother, who died in 1983, and the tomb of Hassan II, who died in 1999. *Boulevard Abi Regreg. Open: daily 8am–8pm. Admission free.*

Medina

Rabat's medina is thriving and surprisingly empty of tourists. Rabati carpets are among the best in Morocco, and you can find them on rue des

Consuls, the only street in Rabat where foreign ambassadors were allowed to live in the 19th century. At the end of the rue des Consuls is a modern handicrafts centre, selling fixed-price alternatives to the medina crafts.

Musée Archéologique (Archaeological Museum)

Tucked away behind the Mosquée As-Sounna, Rabat's archaeology museum contains Morocco's greatest Roman treasures, in particular the *Salle des Bronzes* – an impressive collection of bronze statues from Volubilis, including a 2,000-year-old bust of Juba II, a muscular charioteer and a lifelike bronze dog, ready to pounce on a Roman postman. In the main hall stands a magnificent marble statue of Juba's son Ptolemy, surrounded by collections of coins, skeletons and Islamic tombstones.
Rue Brihi. Tel: (037) 70 19 19.
Open: 9am–4pm. Closed: Tue.
Admission charge.

Salé

Across the Oued Bou Regreg is Rabat's twin sister, Salé. This was once the more important town, but since 1912 it has been somewhat excluded from the business of the capital. Wander through the ornamental Bab Mrisa, unusually high to allow ships to sail into the town (the channel has long since silted up), to the medina and numerous pottery stalls. At the back of the medina is the Grande Mosquée (Great Mosque) and médersa,

built by El Hassan in 1341. The view from the médersa roof across the estuary to Rabat is well worth the detour.
2km (1¹/₄ miles) east of Rabat. Médersa open: daily 9am–3pm. Admission charge.

Ville Nouvelle

The French-built Ville Nouvelle (New Town) is the headquarters of Morocco's government, including the Parliament building on avenue Mohammed V, and numerous foreign embassies. Just opposite the Parliament, Hotel Balima was Morocco's first European-style hotel (1932) and is still the scene of political intrigue.

Planned as the tallest minaret in the world, the Tour Hassan was abandoned on the sultan's death in 1199

THE ATLANTIC COAST

Apart from the expanding conurbations of Rabat and Casablanca, the Atlantic coast of central Morocco is relatively underdeveloped. The exclusive beach resorts in the environs of Rabat, Portuguese El-Jadida and sleepy fishing ports are the major attractions outside the two great cities.

Azemmour

A small white medina perched on the banks of the Oum er Rbia, Azemmour was once an important fishing port that has now slipped into peaceful obscurity, making it a very pleasant and rewarding excursion from El-Jadida. The terrace around the ramparts of the kasbah offers views back towards Casablanca. Stretching south from the town, Azemmour's long sandy beach is excellent.

16km (10 miles) north of El-Jadida, 80km (50 miles) south of Casablanca. Souk: Tue.

El-Jadida

It took 40 years for Portuguese warships to capture this strategic port in the 16th century. They stayed a further 200 years until 1769, leaving a style of architecture which is unique in Morocco. The town's sand-coloured medina is laid out in a grid, unlike the irregular streets of Arab medinas. Here the Portuguese cistern is the main attraction, on the left of the main street – a subterranean reservoir built with elegant arches supported by 25 columns. The tiled floor is lined with lead, which is still impermeable after 480 years – pools of water cast magical reflections of the vaulted arcades. Orson Welles fell in love with the cavernous vault and filmed part of his *Othello* here in 1949. Outside, a gate to the left of the medina entrance leads up to the wide Portuguese battlements and a ten-minute circular walk high above the medina and the Atlantic.

96km (60 miles) south of Casablanca. Portuguese cistern, rue Mohammed al Ahchemi Bahbah. Open: daily 9am–1pm & 3–6.30pm. Admission charge.

Forêt de la Mamora

North of Rabat is a vast forest of eucalyptus and cork oak; note that the bark has been stripped from the oak to make wine corks. Paths criss-cross the forest, which provides an attractive alternative to beach relaxation. Walking and picnicking are its traditional pursuits.

Mohammedia

A large petroleum port and a white sand beach make Mohammedia a somewhat schizophrenic place. Petrochemical refineries mushroom along the shore, but this does not seem to deter upmarket holidaymakers from enjoying the chic restaurants, clubs and 18-hole golf course.

28km (17 miles) north of Casablanca.

Oualidia

This fishing village is famous for its oysters, which are farmed in the shallow waters created by a series of small offshore islands. The lagoon beach is pretty and the waters here are the safest on the Atlantic coast. A birdwatching paradise, the salt marshes provide excellent breeding grounds for numerous species, including flamingos (*see p135*). *76km (47 miles) south of El-Jadida. Souk: Sat.*

Rabat beaches

This stretch of Atlantic coastline boasts some of Morocco's most exclusive beaches. South of Rabat, **Temara** and **Skhirat-Plage** are the most popular and exclusive, with plenty of restaurants, hotels and nightclubs. Skhirat is also home to King Hassan's summer palace. These are safer waters for swimming than the northern shores of Rabat,

but beware – Atlantic currents are treacherous.

North of Rabat is the chic **Plage des Nations**, an awe-inspiring sweep of sand stretching as far as the eye can see. Just before the beach are the **Jardins Exotiques** (*open: daily 9am–6.30pm; admission charge*), which were created by a French horticulturist during the 1950s to display plants from Africa and Asia. Two paths can be followed through the Brazilian rainforest, Japanese shrubbery, and into tropical bamboo groves. The place is somewhat dilapidated, but charming nonetheless. *Temara 16km (10 miles) south, Skhirat 26km (16 miles) south. Plage des Nations/ Jardins Exotiques 12km (7 miles) north.*

Central plains, Moyen Atlas and the Atlantic coast

Watery shadows beneath the magical vaults of El-Jadida's Portuguese cistern

Marrakech and Haut Atlas

The city of Marrakech and the High Atlas are among the most popular and exotic of Moroccan destinations. This is Berber country and the indigenous beliefs and customs flavour the behaviour of the locals to this day. Their religion is Islam but in a mystical form that is riddled with local superstition.

Marrakech gave Morocco its name. It is the beating heart of Morocco. The pinkish red sandstone of its walls is often described as the lifeblood of the nation. Red paint on the walls dulls the blinding reflection of the harsh midday sun, so it has a practical function as well as being a traditional symbol of the city.

Marrakech is one of the world's great cities, a place of legend that, despite its popularity as a tourist destination, still manages to remain charged with mystery. Just a short flight from Europe, the true wonder of Marrakech is that it is a city that seems still to have one foot in the medieval world. Souks, mysticism and magic abound, and its famous central square, Jemaa el Fna, transforms at nightfall into a unique carnival of street performance. The Moroccan buskers are musicians, dancers, jugglers, fortune-tellers, snake-charmers, henna tattooists and magic men. The balmy air is filled with the exotic aromas of Moroccan cuisine that waft enticingly from the food hawkers' stalls. It is an unforgettable experience.

The surrounding countryside – the flat plain of Oued Tensift, fed by streams originating in the High Atlas,

and the great mountains themselves, towering over the whole of North Africa – provides an unforgettable backdrop to the most sophisticated city in Africa.

The mountains soaring skywards behind Marrakech are named after the giant Atlas, the last of the Titans defeated by the Greek gods in their battle for the world. As his punishment Atlas was banished to beyond the western horizon, where he was to hold up the heavens with his shoulders. Legend also states that Perseus came across the giant when returning from slaying the Medusa. When Atlas refused him food and lodging, Perseus turned the truculent giant to stone by showing him the freshly severed head of the Medusa, thus forming the mountains you see today.

The area is still a world apart from the rest of Morocco. The Berber villages clinging to mountainsides seem to have changed little in centuries. Life is hard, with a precarious living scraped from sheep farming and meagre cultivation. But the mountain Berbers are among the friendliest and most colourful in Morocco, appreciating and thriving on the stunning beauty of their surroundings. This is a world only relatively recently entered by tourists, and the Moroccan government is keen to preserve its fragile ecology and traditions. Every visitor has a responsibility to do the same.

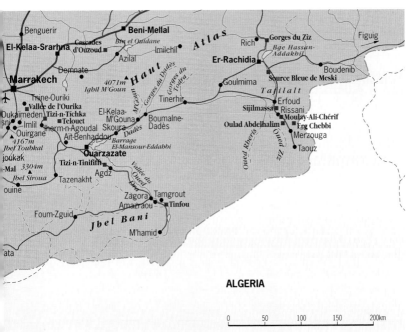

MARRAKECH

Marrakech is a city of the south, founded by the Almoravid Berbers of the Western Sahara in 1062. It soon became the capital of their kingdom, and subsequently, under the Almohad king Yacoub el Mansour, the capital of an empire stretching from Spain to Libya and Timbuktu. Under Merenid rule, Fès took over the mantle of royal capital and the rivalry between these two ancient capitals continues to this day.

Compared with the Arabic elegance of Fès, Marrakech has few monuments. Distinctly African in character, with its dry heat, myriad of palm trees and deep red walls, it is a place to feel rather than see, to experience rather than visit. For many it is the most memorable part of a trip to Morocco.

Marrakech is one of Africa's most luxurious boom towns, with tourism and real-estate development on the increase. Yet the age-old mystery remains. As the sun sets over Jemaa el Fna (*see below*), rhythms and sounds float in the air that have been alive for a thousand years.

Marrakech Tourist Office: place Abdelmoumen Ben Ali Guéliz.
Tel: (024) 43 61 31.

Dar Si Saïd Museum

This museum was once the palace of Si Saïd, son of the family that ruled Marrakech at the turn of the 20th century. He was famous for his idiocy, and the family built connecting tunnels from their Al Bahia palace specifically to keep an eye on him.

At the end of the museum entrance way is a stone basin dating from 1007, which was brought by Sultan Ben Youssef from Córdoba in Spain. Inside are the usual collections of copper and pottery, enhanced by stunning displays of Atlas carpets. The complex dark Azilal rugs are the most impressive, decorated in bizarre geometrical shapes, along with red rugs from Chicaoua. Also of interest are carved fairground swings used at local *moussem* (festivals) until the 1940s, the display of Berber jewellery, and Berber burnous and woollen boots, strangely reminiscent of Mexican costumes. Upstairs is a replica of a bridal chamber, including the gaudy marriage chair.

East of rue Zitoun el Jdid.
Tel: (024) 38 95 64.
Open: 9am–12.15pm & 3–6pm.
Closed: Tue. Admission charge.

Guéliz

Guéliz, Marrakech's French-built new town, is livelier than most. Avenue Mohammed V is full of bars, cafés and restaurants, while the covered market brims with fruit and vegetables. Most of the major tourist hotels are out in Guéliz.

Jemaa el Fna

The Jemaa el Fna is the heart of Marrakech, and some would say of Morocco. Nowhere else in North Africa possesses the same hypnotic enchantment, the buzz of thronging crowds, the riot of colour, smell and sound, and the sense of being on the edge of a private ritual. The vast square, ringed by cafés and grill restaurants, is home to the best of Morocco's street entertainers. From mid-morning, when itinerant orange-juice merchants wheel their barrows to surround the square, and acrobats and musicians take their accustomed places, the Jemaa is pure theatre. Monkeys leap, snakes hiss, drums clash and children box. As dusk falls, the centre of the square becomes a huge open-air restaurant, with dozens of food stands serving anything from goat's head soup to fried testicles, or simple but delicious *harira* (*see p168*).

Tiny gaslights sway, enhancing the ethereal atmosphere. At night the dancers and musicians come into their own, surrounded by small knots of onlookers. The next morning it all begins again.

Paradoxically, Jemaa el Fna means 'assembly of the dead', referring to executions which took place here in the 13th century. Yet the most alive place in Morocco is in no danger of extinction. Giving money to the various entertainers is essential, for they are performing as in any theatre. Snake-charmers make their money through charging for photographs, as do the colourful water-sellers. Without this money there would be no Jemaa el Fna. *200m (220yd) east of the Koutoubia.*

Snails for sale in the Jemaa el Fna

A hive of activity, Jemaa el Fna

Koubba el Badiyin

The only surviving building of
Almoravid Marrakech, discovered in
1947, this small domed structure seems
inconsequential until you realise it was
the prototype for every other edifice in
Morocco. Constructed in the early 1100s,
its keyhole arches, geometric battlements
and decorative carvings were the first in
Morocco and are still used today.
South of the Mosquée Ben Youssef. Open:
daily 9am–6.30pm. Admission charge.

Koutoubia Minaret

This lone minaret is the spiritual
guardian of Marrakech, overlooking

the mortal chaos of the Jemaa el Fna.
Legend decrees that when it was built
it bled its spirit into the city, which
is why all walls and houses in the
medina are the colour of the
Koutoubia. It was begun in 1158
and is the model for all minarets
throughout Morocco – 1:5 ratio
of width to height – although none
surpasses its simple elegance. It is said
the three balls on top were donated
by the wife of Yacoub el Mansour,
who melted down her jewellery as
penance after eating three grapes
during Ramadan.
Southeast end of avenue Mohammed V.

MARRAKECH GARDENS

When the dry heat of summer gets too much, there is no better way to seek shade and inertia than heading to one of Marrakech's beautiful gardens. Do as the Marrakechis do: buy a picnic from the covered market on Mohammed V, take a horse and carriage, and find your olive tree.

Aguedal

The Aguedal gardens comprise 3km (2 miles) of olive groves, nourished by a system of underground channels that extends to the Ourika river in the High Atlas. The original gardens were constructed in the 12th century by the Almohads, but the present vista was created in the 19th century by Sultan Abder Rahman, who transformed the park into a working farm. Later rulers built small pavilions or *menzeh* here for their harems. The heart of the gardens is the pool of Sahraj el Hana, the 'pool of health'. It failed to live up to its name for Sultan Sidi Mohammed in 1873 – his steamboat capsized in the pool, drowning him and his son. A previous sultan had died here in 1672 – Moulay Rachid forgot to duck under an orange tree and was decapitated as his horse galloped on.

Today the orange groves and olives are the courting grounds for young Marrakechis inspired by the view south to the High Atlas.

Rue de Bab Ahmar.
Open: daily, sunrise to sunset.
Admission free.

Hotel La Mamounia

The immaculate gardens of the Hotel La Mamounia are easily accessible for the price of a mint tea on the terrace. Originally designed by the Saadians and

The Koutoubia, the model for all other Moroccan minarets

Marrakech and Haut Atlas

embellished by the Alaouites in the 18th century, these beautiful gardens combine European formality with the traditional Moroccan taste for alleyways and flowering shrubs. Winston Churchill and George Bush have strolled these shady lanes. The hotel has recently undergone major renovation.
Hotel La Mamounia, avenue Bab Jdid. Tel: (024) 38 86 00.

Majorelle

One of the most visually stunning sights in Morocco is hidden away in a residential quarter to the north of Marrakech. The Jardin Majorelle is a subtropical paradise of bamboo, palms and cactus created by French artist Louis Majorelle. Having fallen into disrepair after the painter's death in 1926, the gardens were bought by the late French fashion designer Yves Saint Laurent in 1978, whose villa next door is closed to the public. Fully restored, Majorelle's studio has been converted into an erratically open Islamic art museum. But it is the exterior of the house that catches the eye – painted bright aquamarine, in contrast with the deep foliage, casting magical reflections in the surrounding pools of goldfish. A perfect place to spend a sweltering afternoon.
Avenue Yacoub. Open: daily, Oct–May 8am–5pm; June–Sept 8am–6pm. Admission charge.

Parc Menara

At sunset, when the line of the High Atlas deepens into purple and swallows

Lengthening shadows on the ornamental *menzeh* pavilion of the Parc Menara

shriek through the sky, the Menara gardens must be one of the most gentle places on earth. They are designed around a central pool, founded by the Almohads but redeveloped by Sultan Sidi Mohammed before his untimely end in the Aguedal basin (*see p91*). He constructed the small *menzeh* pavilion that is used in so many publicity shots of Marrakech. The pavilion can be visited, but greater pleasure is found in simply sitting and enjoying the view – the green-tiled pavilion set against palm trees and sweep of the giant Toubkal range in the background. This is the favourite picnic ground for Marrakechis, and at weekends and evenings in summer the rows of olives are dotted with family groups feasting off great checked tablecloths.

Avenue de la Menara, southwest of Hotel La Mamounia. Open: daily 5am–6.30pm. Admission free (but admission charge for menzeh *pavilion).*

The Saadian Médersa Ben Youssef was designed to house over 900 students

Médersa and Mosquée Ben Youssef

Originally a Merenid college, the médersa was completely rebuilt by the Saadians in 1564, making it the largest in Morocco. It could hold up to 900 students, and the sense of space is remarkable after the congested colleges of Fès. The Saadians loved decoration and little is left unadorned. The central courtyard is flanked by high teaching rooms leading to the decorative *mihrab*. Next door, the green-roofed mosque is closed to non-Muslims.

East of rue Baroudienne. Open: daily 9am–6pm. Admission charge.

Palais El Badi

Once the most lavish palace in Africa, El Badi, 'The Incomparable', was built by the great Saadian sultan Ahmed el Mansour. On its state opening in 1603 the sultan asked his jester what he thought of his project. 'It will make a fine ruin,' replied the fool. One hundred days later the sultan was dead and the palace looted and destroyed. Moulay Ismaïl spent 12 years stripping it bare of treasures for his own palatial complex in Meknès. There is little left: a huge courtyard, a central pool and four sunken gardens. In the southern corner is a series of caverns, once slaves'

Stunning mosaic in the courtyard of the El Badi Palace

quarters and used until the last century as a prison. The immense size of the red palace walls and the serene emptiness of the courtyard still impress today. It is not difficult to imagine past luxury, when the palace rooms spread for miles, their walls and ceilings encrusted with gold from Timbuktu.

This is the spectacular setting for the annual Marrakech Folk Festival (*see Festivals, p16*).

Bab Berrima. Open: daily 8.30am–noon & 2.30–6pm. Admission charge.

Palais Al Bahia

Al Bahia, 'The brilliant', was built by Si Ahmed Ben Moussa, brother of Si Said, who started life as a slave and became grand vizier in 1894. Approached along a path of palm and orange trees, the palace is centred on a large courtyard, adorned with two fountains marking

the vizier's harem. In the surrounding dark rooms cedar ceilings and a magnificent stained-glass window hint at past elegance. A fireplace was added by French governor Marshal Lyautey, who made Al Bahia his residence. From the courtyard a gate leads to a pretty Andalusian garden and pavilions. Only a third of the palace is left: the moment the vizier died, the sultan's guards stripped the body and the palace, leaving nothing but the great building.

Signposted from rue Zitoun el Jdid. Open: daily 8.30am–noon & 2.30–6.30pm. Admission charge.

Palais Dar el Bacha

T'hami el Glaoui was Pasha of Marrakech during the French occupation – thanks in part to French patronage from 1920 until Moroccan independence. His palace was renowned for its lavish hospitality: the pasha counted Churchill and Roosevelt among his friends. 'Nothing was impossible,' wrote one historian – drugs, champagne, even prostitutes, were said to be offered to guests. After his death in 1956 Marrakechis demonstrated their hatred for the pasha by storming the palace and lynching his supporters (*see p107*).

The palace is closed to visitors. There are plans to make it a museum, but while the pasha is remembered many locals prefer the gates to remain shut.

Corner of rue de Bab Doukkala and rue Dar el Glaoui.

Souks

Not as spectacular as the souks of Fès, these cluttered streets possess a vitality that sets them apart from all others in Morocco. The sights and scents are African: carpets from the southern oasis towns, silver from the pre-Sahara and lizards from the *hamada* (desert plateaux). Hedgehogs, a country delicacy, grace the stalls of Rhaba Kediam, the apothecaries' square (*see p147*).

Tombeaux Saadiens (Saadian Tombs)

Having destroyed the neighbouring El Badi Palace, Moulay Ismaïl baulked at desecrating the connecting tombs of the great Saadian princes. He is said to have seen ghosts as he surveyed the tombs one night, and immediately had the graveyard sealed inside towering walls.

The tombs remained hidden until a French aerial survey in 1917 revealed the collection of buildings obscured beneath a jungle of plants. A narrow passageway was built to give access without disturbing the sacred ground. Arrive early – crowds are intense (*see p96*).

Place Yacoub el Mansour. Open: daily 8.30am–noon & 2.30–6.30pm.

Once the crowning glory of Africa, the El Badi Palace is Marrakech's most impressive building

Walk: Marrakech Old Town

This walk takes you on a tour through the heart of imperial Marrakech, ending at one of the world's most luxurious hotels, the Hotel La Mamounia.

Allow 4 hours.

In summer set out early. Begin at Bab Aguenaou, accessible by taxi or a short walk from the Jemaa el Fna.

1 Bab Aguenaou

The entrance to the kasbah is unmistakable – a monumental block, adorned with semicircular 'sun ray' decorations dating from the reign of Almohad sultan Yacoub el Mansour.
Pass through the gateway to the walls of the Mosquée d'el Mansour.

2 Mosquée d'el Mansour

This mosque was a contemporary of the Koutoubia, finished in 1190. Now restored by King Hassan to its original Almohad glory, the minaret seems almost modern and excessively gaudy. In fact the bright *Zellij* tiles would also have covered both the Koutoubia and the Tour Hassan in Rabat.
Head right along the mosque walls for 20m (22yd), past boutiques to the narrow passage leading to the Saadian Tombs.

3 Tombeaux Saadiens

Set in fragrant gardens, this small necropolis is a haven of intimacy. First on the left is a richly decorated prayer hall, containing several small tombs. The central masterpiece of the garden is the mausoleum of Ahmed el Mansour. Surrounded by 12 columns and crowned by a fantastically carved dome, it is a fitting resting place for el Debhi, 'the Golden One'. His tomb lies in the middle, flanked by his son and grandson. The other domed *koubba* houses el Mansour's mother and Sultan Moulay Yazid, who died in 1792.
Walk back to Bab Aguenaou on your left, then north 200m (220yd) to a small roundabout. Here turn right and walk 400m (440yd) to place des Ferblantiers, pass through an arch and head for the entrance of the El Badi.

4 Palais El Badi

Constructed by Saadian sultan Ahmed el Mansour, this was once one of the finest palaces in the world. While travelling in Italy, French philosopher Montaigne saw craftsmen carving great pillars of marble for 'the king of Fès and Barbary' (*see p93*).

Pass back via place des Ferblantiers, through the arch on the left and north 400m (440yd) to Jemaa el Fna.

5 Jemaa el Fna

Jemaa el Fna is the meeting place for the city's best entertainers, merchants and pickpockets (*see p88*). For an enthralling view of the pandemonium, climb to the terrace of Café de la Place or Café Glacier and enjoy the spectacle. *Walk 250m (275yd) southwest from the Jemaa to place Youssef Ben Tachfine.*

6 Koutoubia

The earliest of Almohad minarets, the Koutoubia is the symbol of Marrakech

and a building model (*see p90*). The minaret of the Hassan II mosque in Casablanca is a direct descendant. *Follow avenue Houmman el Fetouaki 300m (330yd) west to Hotel La Mamounia, on the left.*

7 Hotel La Mamounia

A former palace, the Mamounia was converted into a hotel in the 1920s. This was Winston Churchill's favourite hotel and his personal suite remains in its original style. Today the Mamounia continues to welcome politicians, film stars and lesser mortals. A drink in the bar or garden is just affordable (*see p91*).

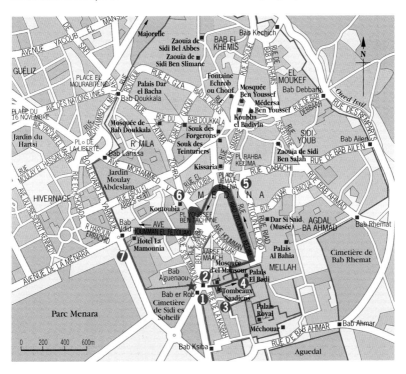

Drive: Marrakech to Ourika

A popular excursion to the villages of the High Atlas and the fertile valley of the Ourika river. The 135km (84-mile) round-trip can last a whole day taken at a leisurely pace. Those pushed for time can make it to Setti Fatma and back in half a day. In spring beware of flooding.

From Marrakech take the P2017, signposted Ouriki, Setti Fatma.

1 Dar-Caïd-Ouriki

The road south from Marrakech is flat and uninteresting until Dar-Caïd-Ouriki, 33km (21 miles) down the road. This hamlet marks the beginning of the valley and hosts a Monday souk. Traditionally it has been the trading post for Atlas donkeys, which are bought and sold at auction; today pottery and hunks of coloured rock are more in evidence.

The road continues 10km (6 miles) to the turn-off to Oukaïmeden.

2 Vallée de l'Ourika

This narrow valley is cut by Oued Ourika, a river originating 3,600m (11,811ft) up in the High Atlas. It is a place of abundant greenery, farmed terraces and fruit trees, populated by villages of ochre stone houses. When the aridity of summer turns Marrakech into an unbearable heat bowl, Vallée de l'Ourika is cool, brushed by mountain breezes. In the past no ruler of Marrakech could afford to ignore the

The fertile valley of the Ourika, watered by High Atlas snows

wishes of the inhabitants of the Ourika: they controlled the water supply to the city. Today Marrakechis flock to its shady orchards and gentle streams. Along the way look out for the carefully constructed irrigation channels, or *seguias*, feeding vegetable gardens. In spring these channels overflow, and stories abound of wily Berbers selling vast tracts of land to foreign real-estate companies, only for the land to be ravaged by floods the next spring and bought back at half the price. In March and April the valley floor is awash with colour as the cherry, plum, apple and almond trees blossom.

3 Arhbalou

The end of the line for most locals, Arhbalou offers a scattering of shops and a hotel-restaurant. There is also a small 'museum' of local crafts, which doubles as a gift shop. The drive can be extended to take in the ski resort of Oukaïmeden (*see p106*), by turning a further 29km (18 miles) up hairpin bends on Route 6305.
Continue along the P2017 from Arhbalou a further 24km (15 miles) south to the end of the valley and Setti Fatma.

4 Setti Fatma

From Arhbalou, Route P2017 follows the river between rocky hillsides coated with holm oaks. About 1km (²/₃ mile) before Setti Fatma the road peters out and a path crossed by mountain streams leads up to the village. Above the houses are seven waterfalls, which,

if rains have been plentiful, plunge into deep pools. Barbary apes are said to live in the surrounding hills, feeding off the walnut trees that shade the waterfalls. Above the river a small path leads up to the green-roofed tomb of Lalla Setti Fatma, the village saint. This is the site of one of the biggest *moussem* (festival) in the High Atlas, which usually takes place in mid-August.
Eat lunch in Setti Fatma or head back north to Marrakech.

Portuguese cannons line the Skala ramparts of Essaouira

MARRAKECH ENVIRONS
La Palmeraie

As an introduction to the landscapes of the south, the palm-tree oasis of Marrakech takes some beating: 150,000 palm trees, spreading for 10km (6 miles). The original trees were planted by the Almoravids in the 12th century to provide shade and protection for crops. The ancient underground irrigation canal, or *khettaras*, still survives, fed by water from the Ourika Valley (*see p98*).

Today, La Palmeraie is the centre of Marrakech's real-estate boom, with hundreds of low-rise apartment complexes, swimming pools and tennis courts replacing the venerable palm trees. A vast modern hotel resort – Les Jardins de la Palmeraie – now commands the northern fringes: where camels once grazed, businessmen now thwack golf balls and the youth of Marrakech go ten-pin bowling in Morocco's first and only bowling alley. *Take 'circuit de la Palmeraie' east from the P7 Route de Casablanca.*

Ramparts

Marrakech is encircled by 16km (10 miles) of ochre walls, built by Almoravid sultan Ali Ben Youssef in 1126. Nine metres (30ft) high, crowned with 200 towers and pierced by nine gates, these ramparts are made of *pisé* – packed clay baked by the sun. The most enjoyable tour around the ramparts is by horse and carriage, hired to the west of the Jemaa el Fna. Prices are reasonable, but agree your fare beforehand. Ask to stop at **Bab Khemis** for its lively souk, and the tanneries at **Bab Debbarh**. Here the skins of sheep and goats are soaked in chalk to separate them from their owners, then left to soften for two weeks in pigeons' excrement (hence the stench). Once washed they are soaked in a solution of oak bark and corn and then washed one last time in mimosa-scented baths. The skins are sold at the leather market held here each Friday. For those less enamoured with dead skins, **Bab Doukkala**, to the west, now houses a modern commercial art gallery (*open:*

daily 9am–6pm; admission free). End the tour with a picnic in the Aguedal or Menara gardens (*see pp91–3*).

THE ATLANTIC COAST
Essaouira

The most relaxed of all Moroccan towns, Essaouira is a magical place of whitewashed streets, wide sandy beaches and a chaotic fishing port, famous for its craftsmen, who work with local thuya wood. The town attracts artists and photographers, as well as windsurfers who consider Essaouira's surf the best in Africa.

Souirah means 'beautifully drawn', and the town has an incongruous European regularity, designed by a French slave of Sultan Sidi Mohammed in 1760. In Roman times, the offshore 'purple' islands of Mogador (the ancient name for Essaouira) provided shellfish dye for royal cloaks. Ptolemy wore such a cloak to meet Caligula and was murdered for his sartorial superiority (*see p77*).

The animated fishing port is the focus of the town. Tourism rivals sardines as the major industry, yet there are few specific sights: the Skala ramparts offer views over the bay and there is a small town museum, the Sidi Mohammed (*rue Derb Laalouj; open: 8.30am–6pm; closed: Tue; admission charge*). Visitors spend most time in the woodcraft souks, marvelling at the designs on offer.

South of the port are the sand dunes of Diabat, once a hippy colony led by musician Jimi Hendrix. The beach is now home to obsessive windsurfers.

176km (109 miles) due west of Marrakech.

Safi

A large industrial port, Safi offers a lack of tourists and impressive Portuguese battlements. The Château de la Mer fortress is a ghostly castle (*open: daily 8.30am–noon & 2.30–6pm; admission charge*), and in the medina an old Portuguese chapel recalls a colonial past. Safi's souks are famous for pottery, but modern industry is centred on sardine-packing and phosphate plants to the south. The best beaches are 20km (12 miles) north of the town. *157km (98 miles) northwest of Marrakech.*

The whitewashed walls of Essaouira

Drive: Essaouira to Agadir

From the romantic fishing port of Essaouira to the international resort of Agadir, this drive takes you along a stretch of Morocco's wildest and most beautiful coastline.

Allow 3 hours for the 173km (107-mile) one-way drive.

From Essaouira the N1 leads out of town along the sea front to join the main N1 south to Agadir; 12km (7 miles) south the 6604 turns right to Sidi Kaouki and Cap Sim.

1 Cap Sim

Sidi Kaouki and the sand dunes of Cap Sim are home to a large domed marabout and one of the world's best windsurfing beaches. The spirit of Sidi Kaouki is said to cure infertility, but most of the camper vans are here for the surf. Camels can be hired for treks into the dunes.

The province of Haha is the western limb of the Atlas mountains and a stronghold of the Tachelhaït Berber language and culture. The hills descend almost to the sea, where high cliffs

Persistent goats search for argan nuts along the road to Agadir

plunge down to beach coves. The Atlas foothills are covered with argan, a strange thorny tree indigenous to Morocco which produces an orange fruit much sought after by local goats, who climb up the trees to feed. Local Berbers grind the argan nut to make a sweet oil – these nuts are 'harvested' from the dung of goats.

The Tachelhaït Berbers have long been renowned for their independent spirit. Even today, if you turn off the main road you will come across villages where neither Arabic nor French is spoken.

Return along the 6604 to rejoin the N1 south.

2 Smimou and Jbel Amsitten

Smimou, 40km (25 miles) south of Cap Sim, offers a petrol station and several cafés. About 8km (5 miles) further south, the narrow Route 6633 heads left up into the hills, past thuya and argan forests to 905m (2,969ft) Jbel Amsitten, and a watchtower offering a memorable view across the Haha and up to the peaks of the High Atlas.

Continue along the N1 to Tamanar; 16km (10 miles) beyond is a small road to the sea and Pointe Imessouane.

3 Pointe Imessouane

This small Berber fishing village has been surrounded by development, but is still relaxed and friendly and is now a favourite base for windsurfers and surfers. A small auberge offers beds and a wonderful sea view. It is usually possible to pay a fisherman to take you on a tour of the rocky coast – pack a picnic, cast a fishing line and snooze the day away.

30km (19 miles) south the N1 rejoins the coast at Tamri and its extensive banana plantation.

4 Tarhazout

The road climbs over Cap Rhir, the last spur of the High Atlas before the fertile plain of the Sous. The beach at Amesnaz is safe for swimming, as is that at Tarhazout, much loved by modern-day hippies in the winter and Moroccan families in the summer. Beyond, the hamlet of Tamrhakht is nicknamed 'Banana Village' for its local speciality, small pink bananas.

From the centre of Tamrhakht Route 7002 leads up into the hills and the waterfalls at Imouzzer-Ida-Outanan.

5 Imouzzer-Ida-Outanan

Once past the banana plantations of Tamrhakht, the palm-lined gorge is

appropriately named 'Paradise Valley'. Beyond, the road climbs to Imouzzer, a whitewashed village famed for its honey (*see p16*). Below the village is a series of waterfalls, which have been reduced by recent drought and irrigation to the merest of trickles. The walk is enticing enough though, leading to a large pool where divers attempt to earn coins by pirouetting into its depths.

From Imouzzer-Ida-Outanan it is 61km (38 miles) to Agadir, back via the N1.

HAUT ATLAS (HIGH ATLAS)

The Haut Atlas is the home of the last of the Berbers who have retained their traditions. It has some of the most spectacular scenery in the whole Maghreb. A favourite area for trekkers, the remote and isolated high peaks of this wilderness region are snow covered for much of the year.

Asni and Imlil

South from Marrakech the S501 begins to climb at Tahanoute, ascending through the gorge of Moulay Brahim until it arrives at Asni, a one-street town that is the administrative centre of the northern High Atlas. There is nothing to see here, just a row of ragged shops, but it is the hub of the region's public transport and provides accommodation and food for hikers. Imlil is a further 17km (11 miles) south along a tarmac and then a dirt road. The change in scenery is dramatic, climbing 600m (1,969ft) along the banks of the Oued Reraïa. Here the valley floor is surprisingly fertile, patchworked with terraced fields where cattle graze. Above it loom the rocky crags of North Africa's highest mountains. Imlil is the main base for trekking in Toubkal National Park, a pretty village, backed by chestnut woods and set beneath a circle of mountains (*see p110*).
Asni: 47km (29 miles) south of Marrakech. Imlil: 17km (11 miles) south of Asni.

Azilal and Cascades d'Ouzoud

Less visited than the Toubkal massif, the Azilal range offers some of the finest walking and most dramatic scenery in the High Atlas. Azilal is the provincial capital, an uninteresting garrison town. South of Azilal tracks lead to the Bou Goumez Valley and Agouti – the starting point for ascents of 4,071m (13,356ft) **Ighil M'Goun**. To the northeast the huge 3,800-hectare (9,390-acre) reservoir of **Bin-el-Ouidane** provides much of Morocco's hydroelectric power (drought has led to a marked shrinking of the lake). Fishing, boating, swimming and even windsurfing are possible from the village of Bin-el-Ouidane.

The most famous sight in the region is the Cascades d'Ouzoud, northwest of Azilal. These 100m (328ft) high waterfalls plunge into a series of deep pools, one of which is popular with swimmers. Surrounding vegetation gives the site a vaguely tropical air. In recent years drought has affected the flow of the falls, but the location is still impressive. A huddle of hotels and cafés provides a relaxing base.
Azilal: 165km (103 miles) east of Marrakech. Cascades d'Ouzoud: 26km (16 miles) west of Azilal.

Demnate

The *pisé* kasbah of Demnate is one of the few southern kasbahs still inhabited. The Sunday souk, held just outside the ochre walls, is one of the liveliest in the region. Southeast of the town a towering natural bridge at **Imi-n-Ifri** carries the road across a boulder-strewn stream. It is a place of Gothick fascination, with the cries of crows echoing around the peaks. These are said to be the embodiments of evil spirits who tormented the women of Demnate, only to be transformed by the spirit of the Imi-n-Ifri spring.

Due west of Demnate is the small village of **Tazzerte**, marked by four crumbling kasbahs. A guide will appear to show you round. About 7km (4 miles) further on is the crossroads of **Sidi-Rahhal**, where local saint Sidi Rahhal is buried. The marabout is the focus of a *moussem* in August – his followers are said to have the power of flight, usually preferring carpets as transport.

Demnate: 100km (62 miles) east of Marrakech. Tazzerte: 47km (29 miles) west of Demnate on Route 6707.

Ijoukak

At the head of the high valley of the Nfis, Ijoukak is the gateway to some of Morocco's most beautiful uplands. About 2km (1¹/₄ miles) south is the ruined kasbah of Talaat n Yacoub, headquarters of the Gondaffi clan. The rival Glaoui clan attacked the kasbah in 1906 when Gondaffi Caid Si Taieb was absent, and reduced it to its present dilapidated state. Caid Si Taieb returned to find his valley in ruins.

94km (58 miles) south of Marrakech.

Ouirgane

Ouirgane is a convenient lunchtime stopover, comprising a handful of good

Oukaïmeden and the snows of the High Atlas

A room with a view in the white kasbah of Telouet

hotels, one of which arranges horse riding into the hills (*see p162*).
60km (37 miles) south of Marrakech.

Oukaïmeden

Oukaïmeden means 'the meeting place of the four winds', a name suggesting how cold it can get at an altitude of 2,650m (8,694ft). The road from the Ourika Valley zigzags skywards with views back down the valley and as far as Marrakech. Oukaïmeden is a ski resort, but in summer this is good walking country. Here, too, is a collection of prehistoric rock carvings: a map is available at the Club Alpine chalet (or hire a local guide). The drawings include lightning bolts, hunters, knives

and a small elephant. There is a minimal entrance fee to the resort.
72km (45 miles) south of Marrakech.

Telouet

The white kasbah of Telouet is a crumbling ruin behind the existing village. It was built by T'hami el Glaoui as recently as 1934 but has been left to disintegrate, symbolising the Glaoui clan's betrayal of Moroccan nationalism, their alliance with the French regime (*see box*). Guided tours must be taken through the great halls and gaudy reception rooms. Ask to see the harem, kitchens and cinema – the caid's brother-in-law was actor Edward G Robinson. On the day of the caid's

death in 1956, over a thousand slaves are said to have fled the kasbah.
21km (13 miles) east of the main P31, 131km (81 miles) southeast of Marrakech.

Tin-Mal

When a Berber theologian, Ibn Toumert, returned to Tin-Mal from Mecca in 1124, he gathered the tribes of the Atlas around him, preaching a message of austerity and piety. His followers formed the Almohad, or Unitarian sect. They amassed to attack the heathen Almoravids, and after Ibn Toumert's death succeeded in capturing Marrakech and Fès. To venerate their founder, they built the mosque at Tin-Mal in 1154. It served as a shrine, but also as a fortress, and was eventually besieged in 1276 by the Merenids, who destroyed the Almohad town but left the mosque, fearful of Ibn Toumert's spirit.

The Tizi-n-Tichka pass cuts through some of Morocco's most spectacular scenery

Today it is one of only two mosques in Morocco open to non-Muslims, holding regular Friday services. Its setting is exceptional, above the Nfis river in front of a backdrop of colossal mountains.
8km (5 miles) southwest of Ijoukak. Open: daily, sunrise to sunset.

Tizi-n-Test

The road rises to the Tizi-n-Test col from Asni to the upper Nfis Valley and the ruined Mosque of Tin-Mal. From here it descends 1,600m (5,249ft) in 30km (19 miles).

Tizi-n-Tichka

This breathtaking pass rises to 2,260m (7,414ft), a serpentine road climbing into the clouds.

THE GLAOUI

'Lords of the High Atlas', the Glaoui clan rose to power in the late 19th century. They controlled the Tizi-n-Tichka pass, through which Sultan Moulay Hassan returned to Marrakech in 1893. Needing food and water for his depleted army, the sultan asked brothers Madani and T'hami el Glaoui for assistance, which was lavishly given. In return the sultan made Madani governor of southern Morocco. In 1907 T'hami became Pasha of Marrakech, ruling from the luxurious Palais Dar el Bacha (*see p94*). As a favoured ally of the colonial French powers, he was known as the unofficial 'King of Morocco' for over a decade. Ever a shrewd politician, T'hami subsequently realised the French cause was lost and in 1955 he pleaded for the return of Sultan Mohammed V from exile. His rule came to an abrupt end and he died shortly after Moroccan independence in 1956.

Berber villages

Historically, the High Atlas is a region cut off from the outside world. Atlas Berber tribes have never been entirely conquered by occupying forces. Yet they are Morocco's indigenous inhabitants, having settled here long before the Arabs from the east. Historians have never successfully determined where they originated – some say in Libya, others the desert further south. Arabic is a foreign language to Berber villagers in the High Atlas of the Chleuh ethnic group, who speak their own Tachelhaït dialects and have a rich oral tradition.

Berber village life is founded on the basic unit of the extended family.

Traditionally, each household or tent was its own republic. When needed, families would band together in confederations to defend the village or reap the harvest.

The Berber architecture of the High Atlas is devoid of the Moorish influences found elsewhere in Morocco: here are simple low stone houses, kasbahs and fortified agadirs, or granaries. Although accepting Islam, the Atlas Berbers also embrace more unorthodox religion, and strange geometric designs decorate houses and gateposts, part of a lost magical language. This is the 'other' Morocco, where women

Berber life revolves around the trinity of the home, the family and the fields

A home richly decorated with local carpets and tiles and multifoil arches

are unveiled, working alongside men in the fields.

In many cases women hold the purse strings, with men restricted to minor purchases. Older tribal law dictates village life, not the law of Islam. At the famous marriage market in Imilchil each September, it is the women who choose a husband, inspecting the ranks of men like cattle at market.

But even in this remote world things are changing. Old black tents are being replaced with shiny, tin-roofed houses; schools are being built in even the remotest areas, and you are more likely to see children with bright school bags than herds of goats. The young are leaving the countryside, seeking a better life in the city. Depopulation of mountain villages is leading to the disappearance of ancient customs and knowledge. One hope is that the advent of tourism in the High Atlas will help preserve the Berber culture – but at what price?

Walk: Mount Toubkal

Set in the wild and beautiful Toubkal National Park, this region of the High Atlas is easily accessible from Marrakech, and is a must for those who enjoy hiking and the exhilaration of mountain scenery. An ascent of the third-highest mountain in Africa, the highest in North Africa, is feasible for anyone of average fitness. It is best climbed between May and October.

Set out from Marrakech early to arrive mid-morning at Imlil. The climb to Toubkal refuge takes about 5 hours. You then sleep the night in the refuge, waking at dawn for the 3-hour ascent to the 4,167m (13,671ft) peak of Toubkal. Descend to the shelter where you could spend another night, or head back directly to Imlil.

Remember to pack warm clothing, even in summer, as nights and early mornings are cold. It is advisable to hire a guide for the walk and perhaps mules to carry baggage. Both guides and mules are available at Imlil. You will need strong shoes or boots, sunglasses and a hat, and sleeping bags (rented at Imlil). Take your time over the ascent as altitude sickness is not uncommon.

1 Imlil

Surrounding Imlil the mountains exude an ancient silence, a world away from the vivacity of Marrakech. This tiny hamlet, already at 1,700m (5,577ft), centres on a wide square where you can hire guides, buy provisions and swap hiking stories with walkers just returned from Toubkal. It is best to set out before lunch.

The track leads through chestnut woods to the right of the village and up to a dirt road leading past the Berber village of

From Imlil the path climbs to the summit of Toubkal, Africa's third-highest mountain

Aremd, dark slate houses clinging to the hillside. Cross the wide plain of the Mizane and ascend the east slopes where the path leads high above the river.

2 Sidi Chamharouch

The white domed marabout of Sidi Chamharouch is 3km (2 miles) from Aremd. This small settlement is a good place to rest, buy provisions and pat yourself on the back. Moroccan pilgrims make the journey here by donkey to worship at the marabout. The strange bare tree before the village is said to be magical and is sometimes decorated with rags.

It takes roughly 3 hours (4km/2¹/₂ miles) from Sidi Chamharouch to the Toubkal refuge on a serpentine path which ascends to a higher valley. At the end of the valley is the refuge.

3 Toubkal Refuge

At 3,207m (10,522ft), this small refuge marks the spring snow line. Very busy in summer, it can be cramped, but the atmosphere is always welcoming and tall tales of epic treks abound. The old *gardien* will usually cook you *tajine*, or pasta. Bottled water and biscuits are also available.

The final 1,000m (3,280ft) to the summit begin behind the refuge. The first climb is the hardest: a steep ascent over large boulders which then turn to volcanic scree further up. There are two paths to the top – the easier of these swings right before following the crest of the range to Mount Toubkal.

4 Mount Toubkal

The view from the 4,167m (13,671ft) summit is breathtaking, literally so if the wind is blowing. The best time to experience being the highest person in North Africa is early morning when the light is clear and you can see as far as the desert to the south and Marrakech to the north.

Descend the same route to Toubkal, and from there to Imlil. Going down is easier.

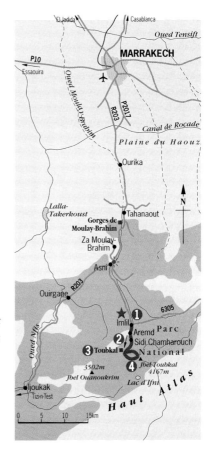

The south

Vast green palm oases, red sand, the nomadic Blue Men of the Sahara and camel trains – the south of Morocco goes a long way to realising most dreams of Arabian and African exoticism. Like all of Morocco it is a place of abundant variety, from the modern tourist metropolis of Agadir, via the red pisé Ksour of the Vallée du Dra (Dra Valley) to the great sand dunes of Erg Chebbi.

While most visitors are based in Agadir, with its unrivalled infrastructure of hotels, beach clubs and restaurants, the real jewels of the south are found in the smaller towns and villages of the fertile Plaine du Sous (Sous Plain), the Anti-Atlas and the southern oasis valleys. From these arid outposts came the warriors of the Sahara: the Almoravids in the 11th century and the Saadians, who swept north to conquer Marrakech and Fès in the 16th century.

A fiercely proud people, the Berbers of southern Morocco have since conquered much of the country through their economic prowess – the merchants and shopkeepers of the Sous are renowned for their business sense. Most Moroccan businessmen abroad originated in this region. The indigenous Chleuh Berber are distinct from other Moroccans: their features are well defined, seeming almost oriental. Famous for their energy and dexterity, the Chleuh are the best acrobats and dancers in the country. The south is, above all, a relaxed place, a land closer to the *joie de vivre* of Africa than the conservatism of Europe and the Middle East.

Do not miss the ancient Saadian capital of Taroudannt, or the striking villages of the Ameln Valley near Tafraoute, with their almond orchards and bizarre rock formations. Travel south down the ancient caravan routes of the Dra and Ziz valleys. If you have time, head east to the greatest oasis in Morocco, the desert border town of Figuig – you will not be disappointed.

Agadir

Once a peaceful trading post, exporting sugar and cotton from the Sous Valley, Agadir is now famous as Morocco's number one tourist resort. Yet few holidaymakers realise that Agadir is the scene of one of Morocco's greatest tragedies. In just 15 seconds at midnight on 29 February 1960, 15,000 people were killed and the town wiped out by a massive earthquake. As rescue workers tried to dig out bodies, cholera spread and it was decided to bury the city and its dead, and to begin again. In the words of Mohammed V, New Agadir is a testament to the 'faith and determination' of its inhabitants and the Moroccan people.

There are few sights. You come here to do one thing: lie on the beach. Fifty per cent of all Morocco's tourist revenue is said to come from Agadir alone. The town is ultra-modern, with relatively tasteful hotels and apartment blocks lining the beach (they are all reassuringly earthquake-proof). The kasbah, north of the port, is all that remains of the old town. From here there is a good view around the bay, north to the industrial quarter and south to the newly constructed royal palace.

Heading along rue de la Corniche, you pass a hillock on the right, now planted with trees. This is the burial mound from 1960, a strangely impersonal memorial to the dead.

Further on is the port and a series of tables and stalls where you can buy fish fresh from the trawlers, have it fried and eat it on the quayside. Agadir is the biggest sardine port in the world, but there are many other fishy varieties, from squid to shark.

In the town itself the Amazighe Heritage Museum on avenue Hassan II has a display of Moroccan arts and crafts.

The sandy beach is the main focus of life in Agadir. Here you can sail, water-ski, scuba-dive, fish, windsurf and ride camels to your heart's content. Or simply lie in the sun for an average of 300 days each year.

273km (170 miles) southwest of Marrakech, 511km (318 miles) south of Casablanca.
Tourist Office: Immeuble Ignouan, avenue Mohammed V.
Tel: (088) 84 63 77.
Amazighe Heritage Museum, avenue Hassan II. Open: daily 9.30am–5.30pm. Admission charge.

The beach at Agadir

AGADIR ENVIRONS
Guelmime

A dusty desert gateway, Guelmime was the last stop on a Saharan caravan route that led from Mali and Ghana to the Atlantic. By the 8th century it was the site of a large market, where West African gold was exchanged for Saharan salt. As late as 1920, slaves were still brought here from villages in Mali and Upper Volta to be shipped onwards to Europe.

Today Guelmime is an uninteresting administration post, enlivened by a 'traditional' camel market each Saturday. In the past this must have been a dramatic sight, with long trains of camels arriving at dawn, serenaded by their drivers. Today, bus loads of tourists arrive after breakfast – the camels are sold not for transport but for meat. Orchestrating the show are 'Blue Men' – Berber desert nomads who dress in blue robes which leave a trace of blue dye on their skins (*see pp128–9*). Most Blue Men are in fact locals, dressing up for the occasion. The camel market does not take place in summer.

199km (124 miles) south of Agadir.

Sidi-Ifni

When the Spanish departed this enclave, as recently as 1969, they left a ghost town of Art Deco buildings, including an Andalusian garden, a Catholic church and a consulate, which still hint at past decadence and colonial luxury. The port is now thriving once more, and the town is a relaxed stopover point, with gentle sea mists adding to the ghostly ambience.

165km (103 miles) south of Agadir.
Souk: Sun.

Tafraoute

A string of *pisé* villages nestles in a valley of oases beneath curious twisted rock formations (*see pp118–19*). East of Tafraoute is a barren land punctuated by oases. Tata is the main base in this exceptionally beautiful region, while 62km (39 miles) south, at Akka, some of the most impressive prehistoric rock carvings in North Africa can be found, though you will need a local guide to find them.

Tafraoute: 144km (89 miles) southeast of Agadir; souk: Wed. Tata: 242km (150 miles) southeast of Taroudannt; souk: Thur & Sun.

Taliouine and Tazenakht

Two stopovers on the main route between Agadir and Ouarzazate, these villages are often overlooked by visitors. Taliouine lies above a deep valley of scattered villages and almond orchards. In the valley is the ruined Glaoui kasbah, a palace guarded by four square towers. From Taliouine, you can go on a five-day hike leading to 3,304m (10,840ft) Jbel Siroua, a volcanic cone dominating the Anti-Atlas range.

Further east, Tazenakht is a centre for carpets woven by the Ouzguita tribe. A small co-operative opens its doors to the curious, and you can see the bold geometric designs being woven.

Taliouine: 200km (124 miles) east of Agadir. Tazenakht: 285km (177 miles) east of Agadir.

Taroudannt

Meaning 'town of the pinnacles', Taroudannt is famous for its red crenallated walls. It is a prosperous market town that was once headquarters of the Saadian dynasty (*see p116*).
80km (50 miles) east of Agadir.

Tiznit

Tiznit is a 'new town', founded in the 1880s when Sultan Moulay Hassan surrounded disparate kasbahs within 5km (3 miles) of pink walls. In 1912 a local chief, El Hiba, proclaimed himself sultan and set forth with an army to face the French, who had just taken Fès. 'The Blue Sultan', named for his exotic desert robes, was defeated near Marrakech and returned to exile and death near Tafraoute.

The town is famous for its jewellery – it was home to Jewish artisans, who began a tradition of silverwork that continues today. North of the souks is the Grand Mosque and the Source Lalla Tiznit, shrine to a local ex-prostitute who was martyred for Islam. A spring appeared where she fell and flows to this day.

There is an impressive beach west of Tiznit at **Aglou**.
*91km (57 miles) south of Agadir.
Souk: Thur.*

Farmers riding into Taroudannt for the market

Drive: Agadir to Taroudannt

This country drive takes you to one of the most impressive architectural sights in the south: the red walls and imposing battlements of Taroudannt, one-time capital of Saadian Morocco.

It is 80km (50 miles) from Agadir to Taroudannt; set out as early as possible to avoid midday heat and to return in the evening.

Take the N10 east of Agadir (signpost Aït-Melloul/Ouarzazate) through the forest of Ademine and the orange and olive groves of the Sous Valley. The road then crosses Oued Sous and, after 6km (4 miles), Taroudannt is on your left.

Taroudannt

The first thing you notice about Taroudannt is its walls – majestic ochre battlements against a backdrop of High Atlas mountains. They are among the best preserved in Morocco, rambling for 7km (4¹/₂ miles) around the city.

The town was occupied in 1056, when the Almoravids conquered the Sous, but remained a provincial market town until the Saadians built their fortified capital in 1554. The walls are made of *pisé* – desert earth baked by the sun and reinforced with straw and wood from palm trees. In places, large fissures are visible, caused by the Agadir earthquake of 1960.

Rampart tour

The best way to see the ramparts is by horse-drawn *calèche* or by bicycle. The

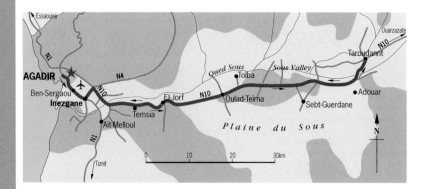

tour takes about 30 minutes, and is most enjoyable at dusk when the walls glow in the setting sun. Bicycles are available from opposite the Taroudannt Hotel on place Assareg and from Hôtel Palais Salam, south of the centre, which is also a base for the *calèches*. Settle on a price before ascending your carriage.

Place Assareg and place Talmoklate

All roads in Taroudannt lead to the two main squares, place Assareg to the north and place Talmoklate to the south, connected by the town's main street. Place Assareg is the hub of action with hotels, restaurants, shops and banks, and a good place to park your car. Some buses use place Talmoklate.

The souks

To get to the souks, take the road south from the Banque Marocaine in place Assareg (the huddle of streets is small and easily negotiable). Local specialities include silver jewellery from the pre-Sahara and limestone carvings influenced by African folklore. Fur hats are an incongruous addition; they are made from foxes, which stalk the Sous Valley.

The tanneries

To the left from the bus station on place Assareg, a street leads north past Taroudannt Hotel to the ramparts. Here, at Bab Khemis, turn left for 100m (110yd) and the tanneries are on the right. Placed outside the walls, due to the aroma of cattle urine and pigeon

droppings used to cure the skins, the tanneries are small and subdued, compared with those of Fès and Marrakech.

Hôtel Palais Salam

A converted 18th-century palace, the Palais Salam hides away against the battlements at the centre of the kasbah quarter. Now a fashionable watering-hole for media types, its palm-tree garden is an unforgettable location for a beer or mint tea (*see p177*).

La Gazelle d'Or

Built for Baron von Pellenc in 1938 as a holiday retreat, La Gazelle d'Or is described by many as the most exclusive hotel in Morocco, located on the route d'Amezgou, 1km ($^2/_3$ mile) south of town. Orange and olive groves adorn the gardens, and non-residents can enjoy a taste of paradise at the bar/terrace, where Morocco's most expensive mint tea is also one of its best (*see p177*). *Return to Agadir after sunset, having toured the ramparts.*

Taroudannt was a stronghold of resistance against the French

Drive: Agadir to Tafraoute

This round-trip from Agadir takes you to the small Berber villages of the Vallée des Ameln (Ameln Valley), and the remarkable red rock of Tafraoute. The route heads south against the backdrop of the Anti-Atlas mountains.

The 345km (214-mile) round-trip can be accomplished in a day, although a stopover in Tafraoute allows more time to explore. Remember in summer to set out early. Take plenty of water and check you have a good spare tyre.

Head south from Agadir to Inezgane and Aït-Melloul, from where you take the R105 southeast to Aït-Baha and Tafraoute.

1 Aït-Baha

An unassuming village 82km (51 miles) from Agadir, Aït-Baha is a good place to break your journey for refreshment. South of here, the road starts to wind into the mountains beneath spectacular ochre peaks, providing some of the most impressive views in Morocco. **Tioulit**, 40km (25 miles) from Aït-Baha, is a dramatic village, dominated by a craggy fortress. This is the domain of the Illalen, a group of 18 tribes that commands the mountain plateau. Beyond, the 1,500m (4,921ft) **Tizi-n-Tarakatine** pass is the gateway to the Ameln Valley.

At the pass keep right as the road forks: the left-hand road leads back north to Irhem.

The blue and red rocks of Agard Oudad

2 Tafraoute

As the road descends you will see the first granite outcrops, a lunar landscape of red and purple rock formed by the cooling of lava flows. These weird and wonderful formations reminded writer Paul Bowles of the badlands of South Dakota, 'writ on a grand scale'. Tafraoute itself is located by a large oasis, a convenient base to explore the villages of the Ameln Valley, and a good place to eat lunch and buy provisions. South of Tafraoute are the painted rocks of **Agard Oudad**.

3 Agard Oudad

Famous for its pastel houses at the foot of the massive 'Napoleon's hat' rock, Agard Oudad is 3km (2 miles) south of Tafraoute. Head a further 3km (2 miles) southwest (the tarmac becomes dirt track) to a desert landscape much favoured by film directors, and bizarre blue and red rocks painted by Belgian artist Jean Vérame in 1985.

The Ameln Valley is north of Tafraoute: head back towards Agadir on R105 until Oumesnat. This is the start of the valley – 27 villages extending 40km (25 miles).

4 Oumesnat

Perched at the foot of the soaring cliff of Jbel Lekst, Oumesnat is a cluster of houses hugging the mountain, including one transformed into a small 'museum'. Most villages in the valley are empty of young men, who have left to seek success in Casablanca and abroad. They return to retire, building new European-style houses among the

ancient granite. From Oumesnat a path leads northwest to the village of **Tamalout**, through the oases and almond orchards of the valley. Wander as far as time allows, as the views become more and more breathtaking – the path to Aït-Taleb takes four hours. In spring the valley is awash with colour when pink and white almond blossom bursts forth among the barren rock.

From Tafraoute, either return via Aït-Baha, or continue west to Tiznit (see p115) and then on the main N1 north to Agadir.

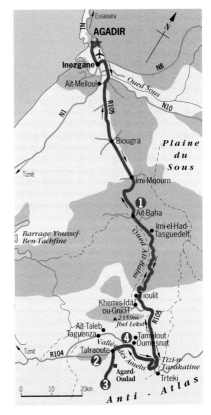

The kasbah of Aït Benhaddou, star of many Hollywood films

Aït Benhaddou

Of all the southern kasbahs, palm-fringed Aït Benhaddou is the most impressive, backed by a hilltop *agadir*. If you sense you have seen it before, do not be surprised. It has starred in six films and numerous fashion articles. The main gateway, which seems so well preserved, was actually restored by a film company. Despite such exposure the village remains relaxed. In the past this was a major halt on the gold route between Marrakech and the Sahara. In times of siege the inhabitants would withdraw to the fortified *agadir* (the *pisé* walls offered little protection – they could be destroyed simply by diverting the stream to run beneath them). In peacetime the valley was farmed as it is today, although tourists have replaced gold as the village's main source of income. Children await visitors crossing the valley, offering to show off their houses to them.

32km (20 miles) north of Ouarzazate.

El-Kelaa-M'Gouna

At the meeting place of the M'Gouna and Dadès valleys, El-Kelaa-M'Gouna is famous for its roses. Here, at an altitude of 2,000m (6,562ft), the fields are divided by hedgerows of rose bushes which in May and early June burst forth into a proliferation of colour. The roses are harvested and processed at the Cappet Floral factory to make rose water, a liquid much prized in the Arab world for ablutions before meals. The dried rose petals can be seen in many of the country's spice souks. The rose harvest is accompanied by a large *moussem* (*see p16*).

An excursion up the valley to the small hamlet of Bou Thrarar leads

through the rose fields, along the side of steep cliffs to villages rarely visited by tourists.
92km (57 miles) northeast of Ouarzazate.

Er-Rachidia

Er-Rachidia is capital of the Tafilalt region, a valley system on the edge of the Sahara famed for its vast date-palm oases. Built by the French Foreign Legion in the early 20th century, it was originally known as Ksar es Souk but following independence was renamed after Moulay Rachid, founder of the present-day Alaouite dynasty.

Er-Rachidia has always been of strategic importance, where the roads from Algeria, Fès and Marrakech meet, and even today there is a large military presence in the town. This is also an area of great agricultural development:

following floods in 1960, which destroyed villages and crops, dams were built and the oases of Er-Rachidia are now highly profitable. The town is a good base for transport south to the Gorges du Ziz (Ziz Gorge). In October the region comes alive for the annual date *moussem*.
358km (222 miles) south of Fès, 510km (317 miles) east of Marrakech.
Souk: Sun.

Figuig

Figuig lies in an amphitheatre of dark mountains, where 200,000 palm trees fill the valley. Historically it has been a stopover on the pilgrimage route to Mecca, a pious but relaxed town. The border and Algeria lie just 3km (2 miles) to the south. Figuig has been fought over by Algeria and Morocco for centuries, the last time in 1975 when

Palm trees line the valley at Figuig

Countless kasbahs line the valley of the Dadès, in the foothills of the High Atlas mountains

border units skirmished in the streets. Today all is quiet.

It can get very hot here and any sightseeing should be done early. Seven *ksour* command the oasis, signposted off the main road. These fortified settlements have fought more among themselves than with outsiders, for control of precious water rights. **El Maiz** is the most accessible and prettiest, while **El Hammam** encloses a hot spring. **El-Oudarhir**, at the oasis entrance, also has mineral springs. Furthest from the main centre, **Zenaga** is the richest and most elegant of the *ksour*.
376km (234 miles) south of Oujda, 385km (239 miles) east of Er-Rachidia. Souk: Wed & Sat.

Gorges du Dadès

The 'Sabre Cut' is aptly named: a steep incision into the foothills of the Atlas forms the gorge, accessible by car along tarmac and then reasonable gravel. It is a spectacular drive, from the moment you turn off at Boumalne. The gorge is wide at first, as you pass a ruined Glaoui kasbah. Palm trees do not grow at this altitude, but almonds and poplars line the valley. As the gorge steepens and the road becomes more serpentine, the rocks are transformed into strange shapes, towering spears and proud mushrooms.

At **Aït Arbi** the cluster of kasbahs lurks beneath a bulbous rock outcrop, poetically named 'the brain of the Atlas'. Further on are the so-called 'hills of the human bodies', with foot-like protrusions jutting from the cliffside. **Aït Oudinar** is as far as most people get, at 25km (16 miles) from Boumalne: it is a good base for hiking. A track leads right round to the Todra Gorge, which is accessible only by four-wheel drive.
116km (72 miles) northeast of Ouarzazate.

Gorges du Todra

A sharp faultline in the plateau separating the High Atlas from the Anti-Atlas, the Todra Gorge is not as extensive as the neighbouring Dadès, but for a short distance it is more spectacular. Take route 6902 north through the Tinerhir palm oasis (*see p125*) and into the narrow canyon, where 300m (984ft) high cliffs descend to the riverbed. The road continues to a small group of hotels cowering under a

vast lip of rock. From here the track leads onwards through a great scar cut by the rock – in spring, when the river is full, this section lives up to its name of 'the jaws of hell'. Here rock-climbers dangle from the cliffs, birdwatchers count rare species and rafters hurtle by. If possible, spend a night in one of the hotels – dusk and dawn are the most poignant moments in the gorges.
181km (112 miles) northeast of Ouarzazate.

Imilchil

North of the Dadès and Todra gorges, the mountain tracks become more precarious and should only be attempted in four-wheel-drive vehicles. From Msemrir or Aït Hani it is roughly 100km (62 miles) north to the plateau of Imilchil. Imilchil is famous for its September marriage market, when the semi-nomadic Aït Haddidou tribe descends from the uplands for a harvest festival with a difference. Unmarried or divorced women, recognisable from their pointed bonnets, choose a partner from ranks of disgruntled men. The village itself is pretty, and offers beautiful walks to the Plateau des Lacs. Twin lakes, said to have been formed by the tears of two unrequited lovers from rival tribes, are the reason for the marriage market – **Lac Tislit** (Lake of the Bride) and **Lac Isli** (Lake of the Groom). An alternative route leads from Midelt (*see p78*).
180km (112 miles) west of Midelt, 92km (57 miles) north of Tinerhir.

M'hamid

You no longer need an official permit to drive to the end of the road at the edge of the Sahara. A dusty town,

A lonely outpost at the foot of the Todra Gorge

M'hamid cherishes its visitors: tours are offered to the 'dunes' to the west. *91km (57 miles) south of Zagora, 255km (158 miles) southeast of Ouarzazate. Souk: Mon.*

Ouarzazate

Advertised as the gateway to the Sahara, Ouarzazate is a friendly yet uninspiring town. The main sight is the Glaoui Taourirt kasbah, a fortress of cinematic proportions southeast of the centre. The courtyard contains a German cannon used to spread the influence of the Glaoui throughout the south. Inside, the ghostly rooms still contain *Zellij* decorations and painted plasterwork, but as the wind blows from the Sahara the rooms seem doomed to disappear under the sand (*open: daily 8.30am–6.30pm; admission charge*). Opposite is a well-stocked Ensemble Artisanal, specialising in local Berber carpets.

The climate and dramatic landscapes of the south have attracted the attentions of Hollywood. Ouarzazate now boasts its own Atlas film studios, 6km (4 miles) north of the centre, home to a plane used by Michael Douglas in *The Jewel of the Nile*, and an army of jeeps that chased James Bond. The studio hotel is open when crews are not filming here. *204km (127 miles) southeast of Marrakech. Souk: Sun.*

Skoura

The oasis of Skoura appears suddenly from the barren landscape, marking the entrance to the Dadès Valley, 'the valley of a thousand kasbahs'. The first kasbah – the kasbah of Amerhidl – is before Skoura village, 500m (550yd) to the left of the road. From Skoura, a maze of paths criss-crosses the oasis. *42km (26 miles) northeast of Ouarzazate. Souk: Mon & Thur.*

Tamgroute

Tamgroute has one of the few Islamic libraries open to non-Muslims, in a

FANCY A DATE?

The date palm is a vital mainstay of the southern oases. Without it there would be no settlements south of the Atlas: dates are the region's most profitable crop. The palm branches provide shade for all other crops, while the tree's roots hold the soil together in fierce desert winds. Palm wood is used to build *pisé* houses, branches carpet most floors and wood scraps are used as kindling for fires. There are over 4 million date palms in the southern oases, producing 100,000 tonnes of dates a year. The best eating dates are found at Zagora (others are used for animal feed). Harvest takes place in late October, when roads are lined with children selling boxes of the succulent fruit. The date palm is sacred in Islam: the Koran describes Jesus' birth among palm trees. This symbol of fertility is often found tattooed on women's hands. Because of its sanctity, the palm is protected: in the past it was forbidden to sell a living tree, and harvesting was strictly regulated by holy elders. Yet times have changed. Recent drought and the ravages caused by Bayoud Palm sickness, a fungus that spreads among roots, has meant that tourism is rapidly overtaking dates as the main industry of the south.

The banks of the Dra river, where crocodiles once roamed

modern building to the right of the main street. The library contains copies of the Koran that are over 700 years old, written on gazelle hide. Nearby, a courtyard of the restored *zaouia* (shrine) is accessible, where the infirm still gather, seeking salvation from the local saint. Down the road is an interesting pottery co-operative (*see p147*).
13km (8 miles) southeast of Zagora.
Souk: Sat.

Tinerhir

A former French Foreign Legion garrison, Tinerhir hosts a large oasis and a Glaoui kasbah. It is a good base for exploring the Todra Gorge, or a pleasant stopover between Ouarzazate and Er-Rachidia.
169km (105 miles) east of Ouarzazate.
Souk: Tue.

Tinfou

The one tame sand dune in the Dra, Tinfou seems to have been dropped there by mistake. The dune only rises 20m (66ft), surrounded by a flat plain, and is best seen at dawn or dusk. The adherent 'Blue Men' (*see pp128–9*) you may see nearby are far from authentic, though.
7km (4 miles) south of Tamgrout.

Vallée du Dra

The Dra Valley is a string of oases following one of the Sahara's great river valleys. Around 80,000 people live on this thin strip of land, farming the rich palm groves. Tourism is apparent but always on the fringes (*see p130*).

Zagora

A dusty oasis town, Zagora has little to offer other than a good base for exploring the surrounding, and much more interesting, countryside (*see p130*). *164km (102 miles) southeast of Ouarzazate. Souk: Wed & Sun.*

GORGES DU ZIZ

The second of the great southern oasis valleys, the Ziz is a mere 80km (50 miles) from the Algerian border. From here came the Alaouite dynasty, still in power today, and during French occupation the Foreign Legion used the area as its main stronghold. Today the great oasis of Tafilalt and the sand dunes of Erg Chebbi make it one of the most memorable regions in Morocco.

Erfoud

As with many settlements in the Ziz, Erfoud was founded by the French Foreign Legion in 1917 as a base from

Choosing vegetables at the Erfoud market

which to control the Tafilalt oasis. It has little to offer other than being a good starting point for visiting the sand dunes further south. **Borj Est**, a fort still occupied by the Moroccan army, provides a panoramic view south to the sand, and north across a sea of palms to the Atlas (from behind the main square, cross Bab el Oued and a track leads 2km (1¼ miles) up to the fort). *79km (49 miles) south of Er-Rachidia, 290km (180 miles) northeast of Ouarzazate. Souk: Sat.*

Merzouga (Erg Chebbi)

Erg Chebbi is what draws most people to the Ziz. From Erfoud route 3461 leads past Borj Est and continues a further 55km (34 miles) to the sand dunes. It is advisable to set out before dawn, to see the red dunes appearing to catch fire at sunrise. (Beware of sand storms in spring and autumn, and heavy rain at any time, which tends to incapacitate non four-wheel drive cars.) An alternative base to Erfoud is the huddle of *auberges* at the foot of the dunes, which provide basic food and accommodation.

The dunes themselves start 33km (21 miles) south of Erfoud, a spectacular sight at any time, rising to 150m (492ft). Skirting the dunes, you arrive at **Merzouga**, with a handful of hotels. West of the hamlet is **Dayet Sriji**, a seasonal lake (now very occasional) which attracts pink flamingos in winter months – an unforgettable sight.

Merzouga: 57km (35 miles) south of Erfoud. Souk: Sat.

Rissani

At the heart of the Tafilalt oasis, Rissani is a windswept, forgotten settlement among bowing palm trees. Its 17th-century kasbah is a maze of streets populated by shrouded figures, many of whom claim to belong to the Alaouite dynasty of King Hassan II. Just west of the village are the ruins of **Sijilmassa**, now little more than submerged walls. For a thousand years this was the principal trading post for caravans from the Niger river which deposited great piles of gold in return for salt and sugar. Today nothing is left.

The mausoleum of the first Alaouite ruler, Moulay Ali Cherif, lies 2km (1¼ miles) south of Rissani, rebuilt in 1955 after floods. It is surprisingly subdued, and not open to non-Muslims. More impressive is the **Kasbah Oulad Abdelhalim**, standing just beyond the mausoleum, which was built in 1900 as a palace for the sultan's brother.

Rissani only comes to life on market days. Then, donkeys mass the small square and the kasbah is resurrected from the dead. On other days, three boutiques sell Berber carpets and jewellery.

22km (14 miles) south of Erfoud. Souk: Sun, Tue & Thur.

Source Bleue de Meski

The French Foreign Legion, tired of dying of bilharzia and being shot at, decided to build a walled swimming pool where they could enjoy a dip in relative security. The Source Bleue de Meski is a natural spring and a favourite stopover point on the road south to Erfoud. The cement basin is still clean, the water flowing freely, but the oasis solitude enjoyed by the legionnaires has been transformed into a crowded campsite.

23km (14 miles) south of Er-Rachidia, 56km (35 miles) north of Erfoud. Admission charge to site.

The grand gateway entrance to Rissani

Blue Men

The ferocious nomadic Blue Men of the Sahara have entered the realms of myth and legend. Today the existence of the authentic Blue Man is little more than a dream – nearly all of them you meet are impostors, dressing up for the tourists.

Blue Men come from the southern fringes of Morocco. They belong to the Rguibat Berbers, a nomadic tribe that used to rely on goat and sheep farming, and occasional raids on the caravans that crossed the Sahara. They are part of the Saharawi tribes involved in a dispute with the Moroccan government over Western Sahara. Some Blue Men would be in favour of the Saharawi Arab Democratic Republic and be active members of the Polisario Front (see p9).

The Blue Men are related to the Tuareg, who live in western Algeria and Mauritania, with whom they often fought (there are no Tuareg in Morocco, despite elaborate claims). The Rguibat wear bright blue robes, the men sporting a blue veil and scarf wrapped tightly around the head to keep out sand. Originally this blue was a dark indigo imported, so myth

The majestic Blue Men of the Sahara, now little more than a tourist gimmick

Many Rguibat Berbers are now farmers rather than nomads

states, by a Scottish merchant to Agadir in the 16th century. The indigo washed on to the skin, turning the men blue. It was prized as a symbol of wealth – indigo was expensive – and the more brilliant the robe the richer the man. Today the blue headscarves are all synthetic. In the past the men would also paint their eyelids green before they rode into battle to frighten their foe. The women are famed for the *guedra*, an erotic dance performed squatting amid a circle of men (*see p157*).

Renowned for their skill with horse and camel, the Blue Men made a good living offering 'protection' to camel trains between the Atlantic and Mauritania. Camels were the lifeblood of the Sahara: in 1946 there were 100,000 of them in southern Morocco.

Legend tells of an American sailor who was part of a caravan of 4,000 camels and 1,000 men heading to Timbuktu. On the way they were attacked by a band of Blue Men – he recorded that only 21 men and 12 camels eventually reached their destination.

Today the nomadic life of the Sahara is disappearing. Drought has wiped out livestock and trucks have replaced camels. The Blue Men have been forced to take to the land and to farm – an anathema to the true nomad. Most Rguibat now live in government housing, scraping a meagre living from the parched land. Some have even become fishermen.

Drive: Vallée du Dra

This drive heads southeast along the ancient camel trail of the Vallée du Dra, through thick palm oases and past crumbling honey-coloured kasbahs.

The 328km (204-mile) round-trip can be accomplished in a day, leaving early from Ouarzazate, lunching in Zagora and returning to Ouarzazate that evening. Alternatively, spend the night in Zagora and amble back to Ouarzazate the following day.

Make sure you have a good spare tyre and plenty of drinking water. Also ignore people waving you down in the middle of the road – a common hustling ploy.

1 Tizi-n-Tinififft pass

From Ouarzazate the road passes through scorched plains for 40km (25 miles) as far as the small village of **Aït-Saoun**. Here a dramatic change takes place as you climb 1,680m (5,512ft) into the twisted strata of the Jbel Sarhro range. The views are stunning.
64km (40 miles) from Ouarzazate is Agdz, the biggest settlement before Zagora. There is a petrol station here.

2 Agdz

Famous for its brightly coloured carpets, Agdz is the old administrative centre for the northern Dra. A kasbah sits on the hill to the east. The Thursday souk is a good place to look for carpets.
From Agdz, the road passes along the Dra river and its lush oases, with ruined kasbahs set against dark cliffs.

3 Tamnougalt and Timiderte

Soon after Agdz are the most impressive *ksour* (fortified town) in the Dra, on the left of the road at Tamnougalt. They are still inhabited by the members of the Berber Mezguita tribe. The kasbah of Timiderte, 8km (5 miles) on, was built by the Glaoui family in 1938.
57km (35 miles) further on is the village of Rbat-Tinzouline.

4 Rbat-Tinzouline

The largest village in the middle Dra, Rbat-Tinzouline enjoys a dramatic setting against the Jbel-Bou-Zeroual mountains. The Monday souk here is especially lively, with vendors flocking from neighbouring oases. A string of crumbling *ksour* encircle the settlement.
After Rbat-Tinzouline the valley flattens and the oases grow larger. Camels graze the scrubland. This is a big date-producing area and in late October the palms are heavy with ripe fruit.

5 Défilé de l'Azlag (Azlag Gorge)

The road narrows 25km (16 miles) before Zagora to pass through the Azlag Gorge. From the gorge the road leads into the vast oasis of **Ternata** and its countless date palms, home to the Arab tribes of the Oulad Yahia and Roha.

6 Zagora

The dusty main street of Zagora seems to come straight from a Wild West frontier town. This is the frontier: the end of modern amenities and the beginning of the *hamada*, the stone desert that leads to the Sahara. A sign at the end of the street proclaims 52 days to Timbuktu from here – by camel. To

VALLÉE DU DRA ARCHITECTURE

The architecture of the Dra is remarkable. Fortified towns, or *ksour*, built of baked Saharan earth, rise from the oases like integral parts of the natural surroundings. None is older than 100 years, but all seem timeless, as if carved by spring rains. The entire population of the valley lives in such *ksour*, spending the day talking in the shade of their walls and retreating to their safety at night.

the south of the town is a volcanic hill offering a splendid sunset view. To the southeast, Amazraou is a centre for date cultivation.

If you have time, head south to the dunes of Tinfou. Otherwise head back northwest to Ouarzazate.

Drive: Vallée du Dra

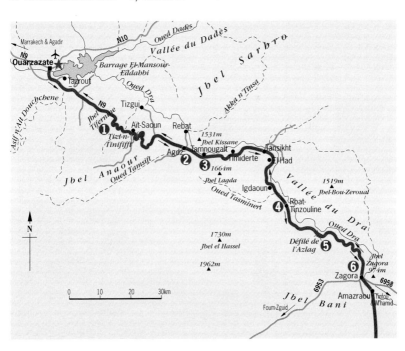

Legends, superstitions and mysticism

'Sorcery is burrowing invisible tunnels in every direction, from thousands of senders to thousands of unsuspecting recipients,' wrote Paul Bowles in his autobiography.

Moroccans have always believed in mysticism (a lot of them have adopted the Sufi sect of Islam), and in rural areas superstitions and sorcerers held as much sway as more orthodox religion. This has led to some conflict with more traditional followers of Islam who believe that marabouts (saints) and their magic powers are contrary to their core monotheistic belief of Islam.

In Berber villages you will still see magic designs painted on doorways as protection from the evil eye. Berber women tattoo their chins with a magical diamond to prevent evil spirits entering the nose and mouth. The orifices of the body are considered vulnerable to the evil eye. Jewellery is considered to play an important role in protecting the body, as are henna tattoos. Gold is considered evil, so most jewellery is made of silver. Amber is protective against sorcery and the colour of a henna tattoo is this colour.

Other protections against evil spirits are the 'Fatima' hands seen on

Medicine man at Jemaa el Fna in Marrakech

doorways or on bracelets and necklaces. Fatima was the daughter of the Prophet. A lizard design gives protection against snakes and scorpions. Large triangular designs on Berber bracelets are said to enhance fertility, as do palm-tree tattoos on the face and hand (the *siyala*). The number five has particular significance in resonance with the 'Hand of Fatima' and symbols with five sides are particularly popular and potent.

The belief is that spirits, or *jinn*, were created at the same time as humans, and every human has a *jinn* double. The *jinn* have fluid bodies and can take any shape, particularly those of household cats and dogs. They inhabit the desert, cemeteries and toilets. One popular superstition is that you should never go to the lavatory between 11.30pm and 2.30am for fear of encountering an evil *jinn*.

The marabouts had special powers to ward off the power of the *jinn* called *baraka*, which means a blessing or special protection. You can receive protective *baraka* from a marabout through invocations and through touch, or through wearing special amulets or charms. *Moussem* are used to court the favours of deceased marabouts who still have the power of *baraka*.

The powers to cure and tell fortunes were essential to *baraka* and

Silver Fatima hands and magical tattoos

many marabouts were consulted for these roles. Medicinal herbs are still used to cure illnesses and as aphrodisiacs. Fortune-tellers are used to predict the appropriateness of an arranged marriage and the success of a business venture. In Jemaa el Fna of an evening you will see medicine men and fortune-tellers ply their trade, as populist mysticism still has quite a considerable draw for many Moroccans even in the cities.

Most medinas contain apothecaries, now more tourist attractions than authentic soothsayers. In rural areas traditional cures are still used. Famous remedies include eating the ashes of a crow burnt in a new cooking pot to cure syphilis, and sewing the tail of a cat into your trousers to prevent sea-sickness.

THE DEEP SOUTH

Since a UN-brokered ceasefire agreement was signed between Morocco and Polisario Front rebels in 1991, it is safe to visit Western Sahara. However, the UK Foreign Office reports difficulties for independent travellers entering and leaving the area. The Moroccan government has poured money into development of the region's cities and the infrastructure. It is a tax-free zone and this incentive has led to the migration south of many Moroccans from cities up north.

The Moroccans fought hard for their claims on Western Sahara. With every migrant moving southward to live there, they strengthen their hold on the region. It is actually illegal now to have in your possession a map that doesn't depict Western Sahara as being part of Morocco.

The landscape of Western Sahara would make you wonder why there was such a fuss as it is harsh *hamada*, which is flat and stony desert. For those from temperate countries, however, this great expanse of rock, sand and not a lot else is a fascinating glimpse of one of the world's harshest landscapes. It offers little in the way of refinement or amenities, and little shade from the sun.

The area comprises four provinces: La'youne, Boujdour, Oued Eddahab (Dakhla) and Smara. La'youne is the capital of the region with a population

Camels gathered in the desert at remote La'youne

of 220,000 (compared with 28,000 under Spanish rule up to 1975). The economy of Western Sahara is traditionally precarious. The Moroccan government has been keen to subsidise the livestock industry – camel meat is successfully exported to the north of the country and neighbouring Arab states. Coastal waters are well stocked with fish and the fishing industry is starting to develop. Tourism is growing, with upmarket hotels in La'youne offering desert excursions, sea-fishing and deserted Atlantic beaches. This was Spanish territory until 1975 and the second language is Spanish, although most administrators speak French. *Check the state of your car before heading south – spare tyre, oil and water. Take plenty of drinking water – up to 8 litres (14 pints) a day per person is recommended. Sunglasses and headwear are advisable. Fill up with petrol wherever possible.*

Guelmime to La'youne

From Guelmime the LN1 runs southwest straight through a series of baked hills. The Dra river, flowing from the High Atlas, rarely makes it this far, especially in recent years of drought, but in Roman times the estuary was infested with crocodiles.

The administrative centre of **Tan-Tan** is a scattering of sandy houses. There is little to see; either head to Tan-Tan Plage, the beach resort 25km (16 miles) west, or continue past into the flat *hamada.*

Further south, sand dunes start to encroach on the road, until you rejoin the sea and a coast of strange cliffs, including an eerie stretch of shipwrecked boats. **Tarfaya** is a good fishing base 234km (145 miles) from Tan-Tan. **La'youne** lies a further 115km (71 miles) south – a breath of civilisation in the desert. This was the target of King Hassan's 1975 Green March (*see p8*) and contains a museum outlining Moroccan developments in the region since then. The old Spanish quarter stands on the hill overlooking a dry riverbed, but La'youne's real attraction is its isolation. Jeep tours will take you into the desert.

BIRDWATCHING

Morocco is a key migration route for thousands of birds in spring and autumn, and many resident species provide year-round attractions. White storks, said to be the souls of distant Muslim travellers coming to their summer nests at Allah's bidding, are Morocco's national bird. There were even stork hospitals in Fès and Marrakech. Little egrets dot the countryside, riding on cows' backs, and on the coast puffins and flamingos vie for attention, while in the mountains golden eagles soar alongside Egyptian vultures. Inland, colourful bee-eaters and hoopoe are common winter visitors.

The best viewing grounds are on the coast and at inland lakes. The lakes of the Middle Atlas nourish wading birds, including avocet.

On the Atlantic coast Sidi Bourhaba, 25km (16 miles) north of Rabat, is an established bird reserve with an information centre. Further south, Oualidia entertains vast flocks of flamingo, while around Agadir are some of the best waters for waders and even the rare bald ibis.

Getting away from it all

Morocco's mountains and desert are ideal places to escape the tourist crowds of the coast and cities. It is a country made for hiking. With 400 peaks reaching 3,000m (9,840ft) and 10 exceeding 4,000m (13,123ft), the Atlas ranges attract numerous hikers. Even the highest mountain in North Africa, Jbel Toubkal, is feasible for those of average fitness (see p110). There are two spectacular national parks in the mountains, while the desert is well worth exploring either by camel or jeep.

MOUNTAIN HIKING

In addition to offering spectacular scenery and good weather conditions, Atlas hiking brings you into contact with mountain Berbers, a proud and hospitable people whose lifestyles have changed little over the centuries.

The ideal time to trek in the High Atlas is from May to October, after which snow blocks many paths. In the lower Middle Atlas spring and autumn are the best seasons for walking.

Gushing waterfalls at Ouzoud

Precautions

Always check on weather conditions, as spring storms and autumn snow are not infrequent. Flash floods in spring can be dangerous, especially in dry river valleys. Make sure you have warm clothing, good boots, and a hat and sunglasses to avoid sunstroke. In the Toubkal massif, where much of the region is over 3,000m (9,840ft), you might get altitude sickness by ascending too quickly. Headache, dizziness and sickness should be treated with rest – stop at regular intervals and take the ascent slowly. Altitude sickness can kill.

Guides

Taking a guide is an inexpensive way to maximise what you see; mules can be hired to carry baggage.

Contact: Délégation Provinciale de Tourisme, Ifrane (tel: (035) 56 68 21). Nature Trekking Maroc (tel: (024) 44 49 77; www.maroctrekking.com). Club Marocain de la Montagne, c/o École

Racine, 51 rue Loubnane, Guéliz-
Marrakech (tel: (024) 30 70 48).

The Middle Atlas

The 250km (155 miles) of the Middle
Atlas range are divided into two massifs.
To the west, the limestone plateau from
Khenifra to Ifrane (*see p78*) is a starkly
beautiful land of twisted rock
formations, oak and cedar forests and
small lakes. Organised hiking is possible
from the ski resort of Ifrane, but the real
pleasure lies in driving and stopping at
will. This is the home of the Barbary
apes which roam the cedar forests in
large family packs. The best route to take
into the cedar forests is the S303 from
Khenifra to Aïn-Leuh and on along the
3398 to Azrou. Also on this road is the
source of Oum er Rbia, Morocco's most
important river, 45km (28 miles) north

of Khenifra: a series of hot and cold
springs bubbles from the cliff. North
of Ifrane at Imouzzer, a string of
small lakes provides fishing and
boating facilities.

Further east is the more rugged
massif of Taza, including the national
park of Tazzeka (*see p140*).

High Atlas

The High Atlas ranges are dominated
by the Toubkal massif (*see p110*), rising
to the south of Marrakech. Easily
accessible, this area offers the most
dramatic of Morocco's mountains, but
is well trodden by tourists (*see p141*).
Less explored regions include the Azilal
massif to the south of Beni-Mellal,
where limestone peaks are cut by
dramatic gorges. Here are the Cascades
d'Ouzoud, waterfalls tumbling from

The barren peaks of the High Atlas

Getting away from it all

cliffs (*see p104*) and the giant reservoir Bin-el-Ouidane. Further south, tracks lead high into the remote mountains. This is the summer pasture for nomadic shepherds who bring their flocks to the foothills of the towering Ighil M'Goun range, the second highest in Morocco. This range is also accessible from Ouarzazate (*see p124*).

Furthest east, the Midelt massif culminates in the majestic 3,747m (12,293ft) high Jbel Ayachi. Fringed with cedar forests, this epic region provides some of the best and least-known walking, although there is less transport and accommodation. For a direct ascent of Jbel Ayachi it is best to head to the village of Tattiouine, where trails begin.

SAFARI

The best way to see the great Sahara desert is to go out into its heart and immerse yourself in its isolation. Whether you take a trip on a ship of the desert or go for the relative comfort of a jeep seat, the desert is a magnetic place that will draw you back.

Camel trekking

In the southern fringes of the Sahara it is possible to take to the 'ship of the desert' and spend time exploring oases and sand dunes by camel. Tours can last from a few hours to several days, with nights spent in the desert under Berber tents. Two main bases for camel treks are in the Ziz Gorge (*see p126*) and Vallée du Dra (*see p125*). Merzouga, near

Erfoud (*see p126*), where the Erg Chebbi dunes (*see p126*) rise 150m (492ft) and stretch for 15km (9 miles), is famous for its white camels and Morocco's largest mounds of sand. The auberges and restaurants in Merzouga (*see p126*) can arrange camel trips. In the Vallée du Dra, Zagora (*see p125*) is the main base for camels – from here it used to take gold traders 52 days by camel to Timbuktu. Tours are available from Hôtel Kasbah Asmaa (*BP78 Zagora, tel: (024) 84 72 41*) into the oasis and to the small dunes of Amazraou.

Remember to take as much water as you can carry – it is recommended that you consume up to 8–10 litres (14–18 pints) a day in the desert. Less strenuous camel trips are available on the beaches of Tanger and Agadir and are always greatly enjoyed by children.

Jeep tours

Rapidly replacing the camel as desert transport, four-wheel-drive vehicles are found everywhere in southern Morocco. Many local travel agencies offer jeep tours of the desert areas. Usually you will be in small groups of up to six per vehicle, and the itinerary will be decided by your guide. It is an efficient way to see sights inaccessible by hire car, and often you will eat and lodge with local villagers, providing an interesting insight into traditional life. Alternatively, you can hire your own jeep – the big car-hire firms have competitive rates, especially when you hire from your own country.

Otherwise there are several specialist companies in Marrakech (*see p88*) and Ouarzazate (*see p124*) – contact the local tourist offices for details.

Mountain biking

Rapidly expanding as a sport in Morocco, mountain biking is popular in the Middle and High Atlas. In the past daredevils have even ascended Mount Toubkal, with their bikes carried by mules, and then hurtled down precipitous paths 3,000m (9,840ft) to Asni, this is not recommended. Several overseas companies run more sedate mountain bike expeditions. Local agencies hiring bikes include:

Atlas Sahara Trek, *6 bis rue Houdoud, Quartier Majorelle, Marrakech (tel: (024) 31 39 01; www.atlas-sahara-trek.com).*

Tourisport, *231 bd Mohammed V Apt 31, Marrakech (tel: (024) 44 81 39; fax: (024) 44 81 65; www.tourisport.ma).*

TOURIST ETIQUETTE

It is important to remember that the Moroccan mountains have only recently opened up to visitors. The environment is fragile and the customs and lifestyle of its population must be respected. Ask before taking photographs, do not hand out sweets, money or pens to local children and take all rubbish away with you.

Wilderness Wheels, *Ouarzazate (tel: (024) 88 81 28; www.wildernesswheels.com).*
Cycle tours of Morocco can be organised by: **Wildcat Adventures**, *4 Marchal Court, Wallace Park, Stirling, Scotland FK7 7UY (tel: +44 1786 816160; www.wildcat-adventure.co.uk).*

Mule trekking

For the less daring, an excursion into the mountains by mule is an excellent way to see spectacular countryside and tune in to the pace of life in the Atlas. Mule treks can be arranged in most hill villages. In

Getting away from it all

Land Rovers awaiting their desert breakfasters before setting off to explore the dunes

the High Atlas (*see p104*), Setti Fatma (*see p99*), Ouirgane (*see p105*) and Imlil (*see p110*) are good bases. From Imlil a classic trek heads up to the Aremd horseshoe – a circuit of several hours, returning to Imlil that evening. From the mule you see Berber villages built into the cliffs, green valley pastures and dramatic, death-defying paths. In the Middle Atlas, Ifrane (*see p78*) and Azrou (*see p78*) offer mule treks, although these are less well organised.

NATIONAL PARKS

Morocco is beginning to realise the value of its great natural beauty and putting structures in place to preserve its ecological habitats. Two national parks worth a visit to get a flavour for the local wilderness are Tazzeka and Toubkal.

Tazzeka

This densely wooded mountain range, 140km (87 miles) east of Fès, rises to 1,980m (6,496ft). In May and June the forest floor is carpeted with flowers, and butterflies appear in abundance.

A spectacular road leads 76km (47 miles) through the park, which is easily accessible on a day trip from Fès. Take the R507 south from the main N6. The road climbs through the Oued Zireg gorge, winding its way to the Bab Taza pass at 1,540m (5,052ft). Before the pass, a rough track leads 7km (4 miles) north to the summit of Jbel Tazzeka and its TV aerial. Alternatively, footpaths lead to the peak and its grandiose view over verdant hills.

This being limestone country, the park is riddled with subterranean passages. After Bou Idir you descend

The Oued Zireg gorge in Tazzeka National Park

Mount Toubkal and the High Atlas ranges

into the hollow of Daia Chiker and a series of caves, the Grottes du Chiker. North of the road is the park's most famous sight – the **Gouffre du Friouato**. A guide takes you through a 30m (98ft) cleft in the rock, down 550 rough-hewn steps to a gargantuan 180m (590ft) deep cavern. This is said to be the biggest cave system in North Africa, adorned with stalactites. Your guide will attempt to break one off for an extra tip – decline if you can, as these are not growing back as quickly as they are disappearing.

From the Col de Sidi Mejbeur the road descends past the normally dried-up Ras-el-Oued waterfalls, through valleys of cherry trees to Taza.

Toubkal

Toubkal National Park is the centre for hiking in the High Atlas. It is a wild place of rocky crags, eagles and isolated hill villages. Mount Toubkal, North Africa's highest mountain, is not the only attraction (*see p110*) – **Lac d'Ifni**, a serene lake in the cradle of 4,000m (13,125ft) peaks, lies just beyond, while east from Imlil the refuge at **Tacheddirt** offers a 3,616m (11,864ft) ascent to Jbel Angour.

Shopping

'Come and look, just for the pleasure of the eyes,' implore merchants from Tanger to Tiznit. It is difficult to return from Morocco without having bought something; shopping is one of Morocco's most enjoyable pastimes, and after a while the hard sell softens and the bargaining game becomes an entertainment in itself.

While the 'traditional' aspect of many crafts is debatable, their vibrant colours and fine detail will seduce – the Moroccan government estimates that 20 per cent of your holiday spending will be on handicrafts. You will need to bargain for most items (*see p24*). Be firm and do not utter a price you are not prepared to pay. If you shop with guides, you will inadvertently pay a hefty commission as part of the final price.

Opening hours for most shops are from 8.30am to noon and from 3pm to 7pm. Souks follow a similar pattern, although theoretically they are open continually. Most Moroccans shop between 5pm and 7pm, when streets are liveliest.

Antiques

True antiques are rare. Beware of purveyors of ancient gold, silver, daggers, rifles, pots, tables and chests of drawers. In Morocco it is best to stick to freshly crafted goods.

Carpets and *kilim*

Moroccan carpets make colourful and intriguing souvenirs, but more interesting are the Berber *kilim*, woven coverings of the Atlas, with their bright colours and bold geometric designs. The craft museums of Fès and Marrakech contain fine examples. Berber blankets and the red and white striped *ftouh* shawls of the Rif are cheaper. Tetouan (*see p47*) has an excellent Berber market.

To get an idea of quality and price it is a good idea to head to the officially run *Centres Artisanals*, where prices are fixed, albeit at higher rates than you should pay in a souk. The Coopérative des Tapis at the Kasbah des Oudaïas in Rabat allows visitors to sit in on carpet-knotting.

Each Moroccan carpet is regulated by the state and given a label: a blue label indicates superior-quality knotting, yellow/orange means good-quality knotting and green means average quality.

Jewellery

Moroccan jewellery tends to be bulky and often contrary to Western taste. As with carpets, it is best to examine quality and prices in a state-run *Centre Artisanal* before entering the fray of medina shopping. Berber necklaces and bracelets, made of heavy metal and semi-precious stone, are popular. Tiznit (*see p115*) is known for its silverwork.

Leather

Morocco is justly famous for its leather. British aristocracy in the last century sent whole libraries of books to be bound by Moroccan leatherworkers. Today leather jackets have replaced books as the industry's mainstay. Leather *babouches*, or slippers, also make an enduring gift, as do high-quality wallets.

Metalwork

Huge pewter couscous pots and brass dishes seem tempting in a Moroccan setting but often become white elephants in the harsh light of homecoming. More enchanting

Spice and all things nice at Guelmime market

A spice stall in the souk at Marrakech

are the ubiquitous silver spouted teapots, although their durability is minimal.

Pottery

You cannot escape Moroccan pottery. Every roadside has its stall of colourful bowls, plates and urns. Such pottery is inexpensive, highly attractive and looks good in any setting. The road from Rabat to Tanger is an excellent hunting ground. More upmarket items are found in Fès.

Spices

Mint is a Moroccan speciality – Meknès is its capital. Saffron is much cheaper in Morocco than elsewhere, and other spices such as cumin, *harissa* (a sauce made from peppers and tomatoes), cinnamon, thyme and ginger abound. Apothecaries sell all sorts of weird and wonderful 'natural' make-up, from henna to Ghassoul mud for shaving cuts, as well as dubious aphrodisiacs.

Woodwork

The thuya wood craftsmen of Essaouira are among the most talented in the world. This dark, deeply knotted wood is irresistible and boxes, trays, tables, chess sets and wooden cups make excellent gifts.

WHERE TO BUY

Before embarking on a bargaining spree in the medina it is always wise to head to a local state-run *Centre Artisanal* to give you an idea of price and quality. Prices displayed are the maximum you would pay. Many exclusive hotels have their own souvenir stalls, and while these are expensive the quality of goods is high, and for the time-pressed they offer an easy alternative to trekking the souks.

THE NORTH
Tanger
Centre Artisanal

For a selection of good-quality craftware at official prices in series of workshops/boutiques.
Avenue de Belgique.
Tel: (039) 93 31 00.

Galerie Tindouf

A venerable antique shop with a large stock of interesting items.
64 rue de la Liberté, opposite Hôtel El Minzah. Tel: (039) 93 15 25.

Grand Socco

Lively food market, selling anything from sharks' heads to Riffian blankets.
Place 9 Avril 1947.

Parfumerie Madini

The Madini family have been concocting perfumes for 14 generations. Customers include the Emirs of Kuwait.
14 rue Sebou. Tel: (039) 93 43 88.

Tetouan
Souk el Houdz

In the centre of the kasbah – the small Berber market where Riffian women sell colourful blankets.

CENTRAL PLAINS, MOYEN ATLAS AND THE ATLANTIC COAST
Azrou
Coopérative Artisanale
Centre of arts and crafts for the Middle Atlas. Rugs, pottery and woodcarvings.
Place Mohammed V, to the left of the big rock. Tel: (035) 56 23 34.

Casablanca
Centre 2000
Morocco's one modern shopping mall, with 30 shops and five restaurants.
Boulevard Enphrette Boignet, behind the Port Railway Station.

Fès
Art Naji
For the well-known pottery of Fès.
20, Q7, Ain Nokbi. Tel: (035) 66 91 66.

Au Petit Bazar de Bon Accueil
An Aladdin's cave of antiques and carpets.
35 Talaa Seghira. Tel: (035) 63 37 64.

Centre Artisanal
Some of the finest crafts in the country, especially rugs.
Boulevard Allal Ben Abdellah, next to the Wilaya de Fès. Tel: (035) 62 10 07.

Palais de Fès
Large selection of carpets, good mint tea and a view of the Karaouiyne Mosque.
16 Boutouil Karaouiyne. Tel: (035) 63 73 05.

The Mysteries of Fès
High-end antiques.
53 Derb Bin Lemssari, Sidi Moussa, Medina. Tel: (035) 63 61 48.

Meknès
L'Art des Villes Imperiales
Well-stocked bazaar, including Meknès embroidery and Berber carpets.
2 Der Hammam Moulay Ismaïl. Tel: (035) 55 37 40.

Midelt
Atelier des Sœurs Franciscaines
An embroidery and weaving co-operative run by nuns.
Kasbah Myriem. Tel: (035) 36 12 55.

Rabat
Centre Artisanal
Workshops on two levels, with good-value goods and a currency exchange.
6 rue Tariq al Marsa. Tel: (037) 73 05 07.

Rue des Consuls
One street in the northeast corner of the medina – the best place to buy an Arab-style knotted carpet.

MARRAKECH AND THE SOUTH
Marrakech
Centre Artisanal
Impressive rugs, pottery and metalwork for sale.
7 Derb Baissi Kasbah, Medina. Tel: (024) 38 18 53.

La Porte d'Or

One of the better carpet shops, with helpful, friendly staff.
115 rue Souk Semarine.
Tel: (024) 44 54 54.

Yahya Création

Lovely lamps and other handmade products.
61 rue de Yougoslavie, Guéliz.
Tel: (024) 42 27 76.

Ouarzazate
Ensemble Artisanal

One of the best in the country, with stonework, copper and Berber *kilim* and rugs at competitive prices.
Boulevard Mohammed V, in front of the kasbah. Tel: (024) 88 24 92.

Tamgroute
Coopérative Poterie de Tamgroute

A small pottery co-operative, where the clay is fired in medieval ovens and glazed with dark green Tamgroute colouring.
Route P31, Tamgroute. No telephone.

SOUKS (MARKETS)
In the country

Morocco is a country of markets in which everyone has something to sell. In the countryside farmers often set off at dawn, arriving at the souk soon after daybreak to shop, gossip and shop some more. On such days roads are blocked with donkeys, cafés are packed, and the town is alive with noise and bustle. Come dusk the exodus begins.

Spices for sale in the souks of Fès

The next day the town is quiet once more, waiting for the following week.

Many towns and villages are actually named after their souk day, an indication of how important the market is. For example, Souk el Arba, between Rabat and Tanger, has its souk on a Wednesday:

el Had Sunday
el Tnine Monday
el Tleta Tuesday
el Arba Wednesday
el Khemis Thursday
el Jemaa Friday (usually no market because it is the holy day)
el Sebt Saturday

Urban souks

In the heart of the medina, the link between shopping and religion is close – the wealthiest shops are found nearest to the mosque, serving pilgrims and often paying rent to the mosque for use of their premises.

Fès
Kissaria

The fabric souk is modern (the old souk was burnt down in 1954 by the French authorities). It is lively, although without much charm. Enjoy the rows of immaculate silk and colourful slippers.

Souk Attarine

Laden with spices, from turmeric and coriander to expensive saffron and musk. Alongside are smaller souks dealing in gold and jewellery.

Souk Cherabliyin

Halfway along Talaa Kebira, this is the slipper-makers' souk, where *babouches* are made (Fassi slippers are the best ones in Morocco).

Colourful textiles for sale in Marrakech

Souk des Teinturiers

The dyers' souk (Souk Sabbighin in Arabic) is a surreal place, where bright bundles of wool hang to dry against blackened walls (*see p66*).

Souk el Henna

Just off Souk Attarine is one of the most popular souks – stalls of henna, natural make-up, strange spices and, so the stallholders claim, aphrodisiacs. In one corner, a palatial rug shop was once the medina's madhouse.

Marrakech

Leading northwards from the Jemaa el Fna the souks are as follows:

Rhaba Kedima and Criée Berbère

Rhaba Kedima is a distinctive square filled with apothecary stalls and street vendors. Once the grain market, it now houses dried snakes, skins and chickens. Opposite, a small passage leads to the Criée Berbère, a small square used for carpet auctions – the famed 'Berber market' touted by guides.

Souk Attarine and Souk des Teinturiers

Souk Attarine at the heart of the medina, traditionally the perfume souk, is now dominated by Western clothes. To the west lies the famous Souk des Teinturiers, where blackened dyers hang out their psychedelic bundles of wool. Just north is Souk Chouari, home to basket-weavers and woodcarvers, and Souk Haddadine, a jumbled confusion of iron, where you are serenaded by beating hammers.

Souk Cherratin

North of the Kissaria is Souk Cherratin, the leather souk, which has lost much of its traditional attraction. This is where books were bound, purses sewn and sandals made. Today there are increasing numbers of tourist boutiques.

Souk Smarine

Beginning with stalls of pottery and spices, including technicolour displays of olives, Souk Smarine then leads north, past dozens of textile stalls selling bright kaftans.

Tanneries

The tanneries – vats of multicoloured liquid, barefooted men, the stench of dead skins – are Fès' most memorable sight, and the furthest removed from modern-day life (*see pp66–7*).

Specialities of other towns

Azrou carpets, carved wood
Essaouira woodcraft, spices
Meknès mint, slippers, embroidery
Midelt carpets
Ouarzazate carpets
Rabat carpets
Salé pottery
Taroudannt stone carving, silver, furs
Tetouan Berber blankets, instruments
Tiznit silver jewellery

Carpets

'Moroccan rugs are a poem, a poem that is never the same, that the mind and the hands play with, but that no machine can conceive' – anonymous poem, Meknès carpet shop.

By the time Muslim immigrants from Andalucía introduced Persian knotting techniques to Morocco in the 14th century, Berber tribes had been making carpets for centuries. There are three categories of Moroccan carpet: the Arabic designs and Persian knotting of Rabat, the Berber carpets of the Middle and High Atlas, and *kilim*, thinner rugs which are woven, not knotted.

The techniques of carpet-weaving have changed little over the centuries. In the deep south of Morocco, nomadic tribes still use horizontal looms, carried in rolls and pegged out in the earth at each oasis. Weavers know by heart patterns that are passed down through generations. Larger carpets will be the work of several people, each person working on a 'field' or section. To direct the weaving a master-weaver or *oustad* is appointed to each loom. The *oustad* has an overall idea of the pattern and colours and will often sing out the colours and numbers of knots, using a

A large selection of carpets on sale

Moroccan carpets, although not great investments, make vibrant souvenirs

different tune for different weavers. This rhythmical song is learnt from an early age and legendary *oustads* are said to have 50–60 different designs committed to memory. In the cities, mechanisation has taken over. Vertical looms are much quicker and designs are copied from patterns.

Rabati carpets are similar to most in the Arab world, with the classic *mihrab* design in the centre. Colours range between blues, greys and pinks. Although sometimes expensive, such carpets are not good investments, and pale into insignificance beside Turkish and Persian equivalents.

Berber carpets are strikingly distinctive and often unique to a specific tribe. Typically, designs will include strong horizontal lines enclosing diamond and lozenge shapes, believed to have magical properties. Others contain strange animal figures, seemingly ancient mystical symbols but actually a recent adaptation to tourist taste. Such carpets would be used to cover the floors of nomadic tents, or hung to divide the tent into separate 'rooms'.

Entertainment

The most common form of entertainment in Morocco is to sip mint tea and watch the world go by. Throughout the country you will see cafés full of men drinking, chatting and smoking (women are conspicuous by their absence). It is said that more Moroccan business is done in the café than the office.

Nightlife tends to be in upmarket hotels, although some nightclubs put on shows of belly dancing and folklore.

Barely a month goes by without some major festival, celebrating local saints or successful harvests. And there is always the world's greatest street fair – the Jemaa el Fna of Marrakech.

BARS

It is not difficult to find a drink in Morocco. Outside major hotels most bars tend to be all-male affairs.

Agadir
Le Club
A gentleman's bar.
La Maison Arabe, 1 Derb Assèhbé, Bab Donkkala.
Tel: (088) 38 70 10.

Corniche Restaurant Bar and Jour et Nuit
Two lively beachfront bars. The former has live music from local bands.

Roof Garden
The highest social spot in Agadir.
10th Floor, Hotel Anezi, boulevard Mohammed V.
Tel: (088) 84 09 40.

Casablanca
Casablanca Bar
Imitation Rick's bar, complete with bogus Bogarts and a piano.
Hyatt Regency Hotel, place des Nations Unies.
Tel: (022) 26 12 34.

Choc'late
Trendy set drink here.
Rue de la Mer.
Tel: (022) 39 85 08.

Diplomat Bar
Plush décor, jazz and luxury.
Royal Mansour Meridien, 27 avenue des FAR.
Tel: (022) 31 30 11.

Fès
Bar Al Mandar
A comfortable, traditional bar.
Sofitel Palais Jamaï, Bab Guissa, Medina.
Tel: (035) 63 43 31.

***Riad* Fès**
The smartest bar in town.
Derb Ben Slimane, Zerbtana.
Tel: (035) 94 76 10.

Marrakech
Le Churchill Piano Bar
Gentleman's club feel; jazz piano.
Mix of Moorish and Art Deco design.
La Mamounia Hotel, avenue Bab Jdid.
Tel: (024) 38 86 00.

Meknès
Hôtel Transatlantique Bar
View from the terrace over the medina.
Best place for a sunset drink.
Hôtel Transatlantique, rue El
Mariniyine. Tel: (035) 52 50 50.

Rabat
Balima Bar
The place for a beer. Crowded terrace.
Hôtel Balima, 173 avenue Mohammed V.
Tel: (037) 70 77 55.

Tanger
Caid's Bar
In the El Minzah hotel. Elegant décor
opening on to a terrace garden
and pool.
Hôtel El Minzah, 85 rue de la Liberté.
Tel: (039) 93 58 85.

Dean's Bar
A favourite for expats.
Rue Amerique de Sud. No telephone.

Tanger Inn
Expat bar, crowded pub atmosphere.
16 rue Magellan, next to
Hotel El Muniria.
Tel: (039) 93 53 37.

The Pub
Food, beer and British pub décor.
4 rue Sorolla, opposite Ritz Hotel.
Tel: (039) 93 47 89.

CABARET AND FANTASIAS
Many hotels run folklore evenings,
combining belly dancing (*shikat*) with
traditional dancing and singing. In
tourist centres large venues are used for
fantasias, re-enactments of Berber
cavalry charges.

Agadir
Agadir Beach Club
'Les Lords' Cabaret dinner.
Rue Oued Souss. Tel: (088) 84 43 43.

Sahara Hotel
Cabaret Al Hambra with belly dancing.
Ave Mohammed V. Tel: (088) 84 06 60.

Casablanca
Holiday Inn
Belly dancing 15 storeys up.
Holiday Inn Crowne Plaza, Rond Point
Hassan II. Tel: (022) 29 49 49.

Tanger
Morocco Palace
Belly dancing till 1am, then a disco.
Rue Prince Moulay Abdullah.
Tel: (039) 93 86 14.

CINEMAS
Most Moroccan towns possess at least
one cinema, offering a regular diet of
kung fu and Indian love stories. Most
films are dubbed into French.

HAMMAM
Every district of the medina has its own
public bath, or hammam. In most there
are separate bathing hours for men and
women, usually 9am–5pm for women,

5pm–midnight for men. In some towns there may be single-sex hammam. Mixed bathing is not permitted.

Washing is an integral part of Islamic worship. Each mosque contains a fountain and ablutions pool where the faithful must wash their hands, arms, face and feet before prayer. After sexual intercourse it is necessary to wash seven times. As the Prophet Muhammad said, 'Cleanliness is next to godliness.' Yet for many Moroccans a trip to the local hammam is more than religious observance – it is a chance to meet friends, chat and relax. For a visitor it provides an enjoyable insight into a popular bathing culture long since vanished in most western countries.

Wearing a swimming costume is best for the sake of modesty although bare breasts are not frowned upon. Bring your own towel, soap and shampoo. If you want to go native, locals use a brown oil-based soap (*sabon bildi*) and a mud (*ghassoul*) as shampoo that you can buy readily in local markets.

NIGHTCLUBS

Most of the major hotels in the big cities and resort areas will have nightclubs.

Agadir
Disco Tan Tan
Hôtel Almohades, boulevard du 20 Août. Tel: (088) 84 02 33.
Flamingo, Agadir Beach Club
Rue Oued Souss. Tel: (088) 84 43 43.

Casablanca
Le Calypso
International beachfront disco.
61 boulevard de la Corniche. Tel: (022) 93 67 15.

Marrakech
Le Club
Exclusive dancing in the bowels of La Mamounia Hotel.
Hôtel La Mamounia, avenue Bab Jdid. Tel: (024) 44 44 09; fax: (024) 44 46 60.
Pacha
Large club with international DJ sets.
Boulevard Mohammed VI, L'Aguedal hotel zone. Tel: (024) 38 84 00; www.pachamarrakech.com
Paradise
Upmarket club.
Avenue de France. Tel: (024) 33 91 00.
Theatro Marrakech
For on-trénd locals.
Hotel Es Saadi, rue El-Quadissia, Hivernage. Tel: (024) 44 88 11; www.theatromarrakesh.com

Tanger
Borsalino's
Smart mainstream disco.
30 rue Prince Moulay Abdallah. Tel: (039) 94 31 63.

SPAS

The curative waters of Morocco have been enjoyed and exploited ever since Roman times. In the Middle Atlas, water rich in minerals springs forth from volcanic rock at a steady 54°C (129°F). Moulay Yacoub, just outside Fès, is an ultra-modern thermal station amid the rolling Trhrat hills.

Opened in 1992, this luxurious complex comprises hot water swimming pools, individual mineral baths, massage relaxation and beauty treatment, as well as four specialised medical departments. A week's intensive health treatment is inexpensive by Western standards, with accommodation at the neighbouring Hotel Moulay Yacoub. There are also more old-fashioned spa baths at Sidi Harazem, 15km (9 miles) east of Fès.
Thermes de Moulay Yacoub, 20km (12 miles) northwest of Fès.
Tel: (035) 69 40 64. Accommodation from Hotel Moulay Yacoub, Moulay Yacoub Autonomous Centre.

Tel: (035) 69 40 35;
fax: (035) 69 40 12.

STREET ENTERTAINMENT

From the cantankerous old water-sellers in Casablanca to the excitable snake-charmers of Marrakech and the Andalusian musicians of Tetouan, Morocco provides a memorable selection of informal entertainment. The capital of street entertainment is undoubtedly the Jemaa el Fna in Marrakech. Here, black cobras dance and trained monkeys jump among Tazeroualt acrobats. Few spectacles rival the scene at sunset, with smoke billowing from food grills and dancers, boxers, storytellers, drummers and serpent-charmers all vying for the attention of the massed crowds.

Entertainment

A Chleuh dancer gives his all in the Jemaa el Fna, Marrakech

Music and dance

'The whole Muslim world is practically controlled by music,' noted William S Burroughs. Everywhere you go in Morocco you will hear music playing, as it has for countless centuries.

Traditionally, there are two sorts of Moroccan music: the simple oral poetry of the countryside, and sophisticated instrumental music which originated in Andalucía over 1,000 years ago. The instrumental music is Morocco's classical music and is usually played by large orchestras – violins, lutes, tambourine and even the odd piano. This style is the most commonly recorded, and you will hear it everywhere. Its haunting harmonies, often a single theme repeating, tell of lost love and passionate betrothal.

The music of the Moroccan countryside is a collective music, involving numerous musicians, storytellers and dancers. In the High Atlas, the Berber tribes gather on

Moroccan musical instruments on sale

Music and dance are everywhere in Morocco, from country fields to bustling medinas

festive occasions to dance to a simple pipe (*nai*) and drums (*bendirs*), forming a large circle into which pass selected storytellers. More specialised Chleuh dances are traditionally a sexual invitation to onlookers, performed by young boys.

Further south, the influence of African rhythms is evident: in the music of the *gnaoua* brotherhood the three-stringed *gimbri* lute accompanies *garagab* (castanets) to create a rhythmic chant, traditionally used to dispel evil spirits. This animated southern music tells of religious, social and worldly themes, exalting love and the joys of drinking.

The most famous of Moroccan dances is the *guedra*, performed by tribeswomen of the Sahara. This traditional erotic dance, in which women crouch low, gyrating their hips as a hint to the male audience, gradually removing layers of veils, is commonly held for tour groups in Agadir hotels (without its traditional finale, when the last garment is removed).

While older musical traditions are strictly upheld, there has been a recent turn towards synthesised music from Algeria – Rai. This 'North African Rap' is the music of the young, and its heavy beat and harsh electric guitar can be heard in most medinas.

The rise in popularity of world music has led to the collaboration of Moroccan musicians with musicians from various other nations to produce some interesting transcultural mixes of sound.

Children

Bringing children to Morocco may not seem like the best idea for a relaxing holiday, but it is a country that welcomes children with endless natural playgrounds, fairytale cities and excellent beaches. Moroccan society is firmly based on the family unit and children are greeted with great enthusiasm.

Make sure that children are well covered, wearing hats, sunglasses and loose fitting clothes, and are kept out of the sun. Apart from these simple precautions there is little to worry about – a Moroccan holiday will be an unforgettable experience for any child.

Most families tend to base themselves in one of Morocco's coastal resorts, venturing into the cities for day trips. The Mediterranean coast is a popular destination, with resorts like Kabila and Smir-Restinga tailoring their facilities specifically for families. For slightly older children, hiring a car and taking them out to see some of the countryside is always memorable. In the cities busy medinas can be overwhelming for small children, but fascinating for older age groups. Ruins such as the Chellah and Kasbah des Oudaïas in Rabat or the El Badi Palace in Marrakech provide eternal inspiration for children's games.

Babies

Moroccan pharmacies are very well stocked. Medical services in urban areas are highly competent. The usual brands of disposable nappies are available, as are baby food and most common medicines. All pharmacists speak French; fewer speak English.

Beaches

The best beaches for young children are on the Mediterranean coast from Ceuta to Al-Hoceima, where sheltered bays provide excellent swimming. The new resort of MarinaSmir (*see p47*) has been developed for families, with babysitting facilities, playgrounds and 3km (2 miles) of sand. There is also a large aqua park. On the Atlantic coast, offshore currents are strong and swimming is dangerous. Sheltered beaches include Temara, Skhirat, Oualidia and Agadir. The beach clubs of Aïn-Diab on the Casablanca corniche are well suited to children, with sports facilities, swimming pools and restaurants.

Camels and mules

Camel rides are always popular with children. During the summer season camels patrol the beaches of Tanger, Martil and Agadir. In the Middle and High Atlas mules can be hired for short treks into the hills (*see p139*). In Marrakech and Meknès, horse-drawn *calèches* are a good way to see the city; they can be hired per hour or per journey.

Caves

East of Fès, the Friouato cave in the Tazzeka National Park provides an interesting diversion – children enjoy finding the impressive collection of stalactites (*see p141*). With a guide the cave is perfectly safe. Elsewhere, the Grotte du Chameau near Oujda (*see p46*) is less well organised, but with a torch you should be able to find the famous camel-shaped stalactite.

Desert

The Dra and Ziz valleys are ideally suited to children, with exotic kasbahs to play in, palm-tree oases to explore and the lure of desert sand dunes at Tinfou and Erfoud. Swimming should not be attempted in southern rivers – many are infected with bilharzia.

Gardens

The gardens of Marrakech are always popular with kids (*see pp91–3*) – the Menara gardens and pool, the Aguedal basin and particularly the Majorelle gardens provide endless inspiration for games. In Rabat (*see p80*) the Chellah and Oudaïa gardens are both equally entertaining places to play.

Health

Moroccan pharmacies are very well stocked and medical attention is more than competent. Take necessary precautions such as keeping children's heads well covered against the sun, drinking only bottled water and avoiding raw fruit and vegetables that may be washed in contaminated water. Health risks in tourist resorts are minimal.

Safari

One of the highlights of Morocco for any child is a day trip in the Middle Atlas to see wild Barbary apes. The drive from Azrou to Khenifra is best suited for an ape safari (*see p137*). On the coast, large flocks of flamingos are also star attractions – try the Lac de Sidi Bourhaba just north of Rabat, Oualidia (*see pp84–5*), and Oued Sous outside Agadir.

Beach 'kickabout' at Agadir

Sport and leisure

Despite extreme temperatures and landscapes, Moroccans are active and passionate sportspeople. Football is the national addiction, while King Hassan's predilection for golf led to the construction of world-class courses; and the varied topography offers endless possibilities for more adventurous pursuits.

Ballooning

In the summer two French balloonists run trips over Marrakech and further south towards the desert. Most balloon flights are in the early morning and prebooking is essential.

Ciel d'Afrique, 15 rue Mauritanie, Guéliz, Marrakech. Tel: (024) 43 28 43; fax: (024) 43 28 47; email: contact@cieldafrique.info; www.cieldafrique.info

Fishing

Morocco is blessed with a refreshing amount of water and fish are plentiful, so there is plenty of opportunity for anglers. Coarse fishing is most popular, with lakes and reservoirs well stocked with bass, perch and pike. Try the string of lakes east of Imouzzer-Kandar, Moulay Youssef, east of Marrakech, and El Kansera, west of Meknès. Permits are required: information from Moroccan National Tourist Office or Eaux et Forêts, *11 rue Moulay Abdelaziz, Rabat. Tel: (037) 76 26 94; 25 boulevard Roudani, Casablanca. Tel: (022) 27 15 98.* Bring your own equipment.

Sea-fishing requires no permit and the Atlantic coastal waters are ideal for surfcasting – mackerel, bream, sea bass and tuna are the main attractions. The sea off Western Sahara provides some of the best game fishing in the world. For information contact Best of Morocco, *38 Market Place, Chippenham, Wiltshire SN15 3HT. Tel: 0845 026 45 85 or +44 1249 467157; www.morocco-travel.com* or Sochatour, *71 avenue des FAR, Casablanca. Tel: (022) 31 47 19; www.sochatour.com*

Football

Football is huge in Morocco. The national team (nickname the Atlas Lions) qualified for both the 1994 and 1998 World Cup finals, but missed out on those in 2002 and 2006. They are gearing up for South Africa 2010. They were beaten finalists in the African Cup of Nations in 2004, but went out at the group stage in 2006 and 2008.

Everywhere you go you will see football matches, from High Atlas hill villages to the beaches of Casablanca and Agadir. A stroll along the beach at Agadir on a Sunday morning will give you an idea of how popular the Beautiful Game is with hundreds of kids of all ages playing on makeshift pitches. Their idols are international players from the English Premiership and the Spanish La Liga, but it won't be long until the names of Moroccan superstars grace the back of their football shirts.

Golf

In a land touched by the Sahara there is no shortage of bunkers, but it may come as a surprise to find lush greens and immaculate fairways. Morocco is rapidly becoming a top golf holiday destination. Former King Hassan II was a golf fanatic, and under his patronage once-barren landscapes have blossomed into golfing oases. Green charges are lower than in Europe and the weather is consistently good, attracting ardent amateurs from all over the world. The top professionals gather each year at the Royal Dar es Salam near Rabat for the Hassan II trophy. If you need further information, contact the Royal Moroccan Golf Federation, *Royal Golf Dar-es-Salam, Rabat. Tel: (037) 75 58 64; www.royalgolfdaressalam.com.* Here is a list of the best clubs in Morocco:

Agadir

Golf du Soleil. *Tel: (088) 33 73 29; fax: (088) 33 73 33.*

Les Dunes. *Tel: (028) 82 95 00; fax: (028) 83 46 49.*
Royal Golf d'Agadir.
Tel: (048) 24 85 51; fax: (048) 33 55 33.

Ben Slimane (near Casablanca)
Royal Golf Club. *Tel: (022) 32 87 93.*

Cabo Negro (near Tetouan)
Royal Golf Club. *Tel: (039) 97 83 03; fax: (039) 97 81 41.*

Casablanca
Anfa Royal Golf Club. *Tel: (022) 36 10 26; fax: (022) 39 33 74.*

El-Jadida (south of Casablanca)
Royal Golf Club, *Km 7, route de Casablanca. Tel: (023) 35 22 51.*

Fès
Royal Golf Club. *Tel: (035) 76 38 49.*

Marrakech
Amelkis. *Tel: (024) 40 44 14.*
Palmeraie. *Tel: (024) 30 10 10.*
Royal Golf. *Tel: (024) 44 43 41; fax: (024) 43 00 84.*

Meknès
Royal Golf Club. *Tel: (035) 53 07 53; fax: (035) 55 79 34.*

Mohammedia
Royal Golf Club. *Tel: (023) 32 46 56; fax: (023) 32 11 02.*

Ouarzazate
Royal Golf Club. *Tel: (024) 88 26 53; fax: (044) 88 33 44.*

Rabat
Royal Dar es Salam.
Tel: (037) 75 58 64; fax: (037) 75 76 71.

Tanger
Royal Country Club.
Tel: (039) 94 44 84; fax: (039) 94 54 50.

Hiking and climbing

The Middle and High Atlas, Anti-Atlas and Rif ranges provide numerous hiking possibilities for all levels of fitness (*see p136*). Local agencies specialising in hiking include Ribat Tours, *6 rue des Vieux Marrakechis, Guéliz, Marrakech (tel: (024) 43 86 93; www.ribatours.com)*.

There are also many climbing regions in the High Atlas, notably the Imlil and El-Kelaa-M'Gouna regions. For further information contact the Club Alpin Français, *50 boulevard Sidi Abderrrahamane, Casablanca (tel: (022) 98 75 19; www.caf-maroc.com)*. For guides contact National Association of Guides for the High Mountains (ANGAHM), *BP 47, Asni, Marrakech (tel: (024) 44 49 79)*.

Hunting

Hunting in Morocco goes back to Roman days when Berber warriors were sent out to catch lions, leopards and elephants for Roman amphitheatres. Morocco's present hunting reserves offer grouse and fowl as well as wild boar. Estates are often owned by travel groups – Sochatour, at *71 avenue des FAR, Casablanca (tel: (022) 31 47 19; www.sochatour.com)*, is the biggest, with reserves near Marrakech, Agadir and Tanger. They will also arrange temporary import licences for guns.

Riding

Arab horses are justly famous for their grace, speed and volatile temper.

Morocco offers exhilarating riding, from the foothills of the High Atlas to the plains of Meknès. The recognised base for mountain riding holidays is La Roseraie at Ouirgane, *60km (37 miles) south of Marrakech (tel: (024) 43 91 28; www.laroseraiehotel.com)*. On the Mediterranean coast, Cabo Negro provides riding holidays at *La Ferma (tel: (039) 97 80 75)*. For general information contact the Fédération Royale de Sports Equestres, *Dar-es-Salam, BP 742, Rabat (tel: (037) 75 44 24)*.

Running

Jogging is a serious sport in Morocco, where personal fitness is a matter of pride to every young male. Morocco is a world-beater in the field of athletics. Hicham el Guerrouj, now retired, is world-record holder for 1,500m. The superstars Khalid Skah, Said Aouita and Nawal el-Moutawakel were all Olympic champions. El-Moutawakel was the first Muslim woman ever to win Olympic Gold and has become the first female Muslim to be elected to the board of the IOC. The Marrakech marathon takes place each January (*www.marathon-marrakech.com*) and attracts more than 5,000 runners.

Skiing

Oukaïmeden (*see p106*), 72km (45 miles) south of Marrakech, is the top skiing resort, open from December until April. It has one of the world's highest lifts (over 3,000m/9,840ft), and offers seven runs, plus hotels and ski hire. Morocco's second resort, Mischliffen, in the Middle Atlas, is less reliable – its three main runs are open for about six weeks each winter.

Off-piste skiing is becoming very popular in the High Atlas, with skiers hiking to remote 4,000m (13,125ft) summits while their skis are transported on mules, and hurtling down virgin pistes. This is recommended for only the most experienced skier.

There are no ski hotlines in Morocco. For information contact the Fédération Royale Marocaine de Ski et Montagne, *Parc de la Ligue Arabe, BP 15 899, Casablanca (tel/fax: (022) 47 49 79; www.frmsm.ma).*

Tennis

With all-year-round good weather, Morocco is a tennis-player's paradise. Most big hotels now have their own courts, usually clay. Agadir is the kingdom's tennis capital with over 130 courts. Most courts are floodlit for night play, when temperatures are more bearable. Equipment can be hired from hotels but it is preferable to bring your own racquet and balls.

Watersports

With 3,530km (2,193 miles) of coastline, there is much potential for messing about in Moroccan water. The only drawback is the strong offshore current along the Atlantic coast – it is best to stick to resorts mentioned in the Destination Guide. Agadir is the centre

of aquatic action, offering waterskiing, jet ski, sub-aqua diving, pedalos and even paragliding. Further north, Essaouira is known as Wind City Afrika to legions of top-class surfers. International windsurf competitions are held here each spring. Other top surfing venues include Tarhazout, near Agadir, Plage des Nations (*see p85*), at Rabat, and Mehdia. For further information contact Royal Morocco Federation of Surfing and Bodyboarding, *Casablanca (www.fedesurfmaroc.com).*

The Mediterranean coast is much calmer and better suited to more sedate aquatic sport: M'Diq has a yachting club that arranges sailing courses in the summer (*tel: (039) 97 56 59).* Royal Moroccan Sailboat Federation, *avenue Ibn Sina, Agdal, Rabat (tel: (037) 67 09 56),* Royal Moroccan Yacht Club, *Rabat (tel: (037) 72 02 64),* Yacht Club de Maroc, *quai de Plaisance, Mohammedia (tel: (023) 32 79 19).*

Inland, the rivers of the High Atlas are becoming famous for canoeing and white-water rafting. 'Tubing', in which you tumble along rapids in a rubber tube, is also popular. For information, contact the Royal Moroccan Canoe-Kayak Federation, *Centre National des Sports, BP 332, avenue Ibn Sina, Rabat (tel: (037) 77 02 81).*

Most small towns have inexpensive municipal swimming pools. Further south, pools are restricted to up-market hotels, which usually permit non-residents to swim for a small fee or if you buy drinks or food.

Food and drink

Moroccan cuisine is among the best in the world. Local produce is nourished by African sunshine, and then spiced by Arab ingenuity or refined by French subtlety to produce a meal that will delight your palate. Most Moroccans eat at home, the evening meal being the most important social event of the family's day.

A genuine invitation to share a Moroccan family meal should not be turned down – this is where you will taste the national cuisine at its best and get a glimpse into family life to boot. Outside the home, a whole range of restaurants welcomes the visitor, from the chaotic grill stands of the Jemaa el Fna to the secluded and exclusive French restaurants of Casablanca and Rabat.

Gourmet palaces to street stalls

At the top end of the market, traditional Moroccan cuisine is served with Western-style efficiency. In many cities, old palaces have been converted into sumptuous atmospheric dining rooms. Small local restaurants offer the same traditional food at lower prices, often in similarly authentic surroundings.

On the street, numerous makeshift grills serve tender mutton, grilled fish, fresh salads, thick *harira* soup (*see p168*) and hunks of bread. You should go easy on your stomach at first, but you will soon adapt to this most Moroccan of culinary feasts.

Strict vegetarians will have problems in Morocco. Stick to restaurants in resort areas. Cheese and egg- based dishes are generally readily available and vegetable couscous will be on some restaurant menus.

Prices

You can eat very cheaply in Morocco, and most meals will cost less than 100DH (dirhams). Top restaurants can charge three times this amount. The following restaurants are listed under four price headings, indicating cost per person excluding alcohol. In most establishments a government tax of 10 per cent is included; 10 per cent service tax is sometimes included but is usually at the discretion of the client.

★ Cheap
★★ Moderate
★★★ Expensive
★★★★ Very expensive

THE NORTH
Asilah
Al Kasaba ★★
Once run by Lord
Churchill, this seafront
restaurant specialises
in seafood.
Place Zallach.
Tel: (039) 41 70 12.

Chefchaouen
Restaurant Tissemlal ★★
Delicious good-value
food in a converted
palace. Set menu.
Can be busy.
22 rue Targui.
Tel: (039) 98 61 53.

Tanger
La Grenouille ★★
Just off boulevard
Pasteur, a 1950s
atmosphere and good
European-style food.
3 rue Jabha el Outania.
Tel: (039) 94 80 16.
Closed: Mon.
Restaurant Hammadi ★★
Traditional food, bad for
entertainment.
2 rue de la Kasbah.
Tel: (039) 93 45 14.
San Remo ★★
A small Italian restaurant
serving good homemade
pasta and pizza.
15 rue Ahmed Chaouki.
Tel: (039) 93 84 51.

El Korsan ★★★
The best Moroccan
restaurant in town, in
the El Minzah Hotel.
Hôtel El Minzah, 85 rue
de la Liberté. Tel: (039) 93
58 85. Closed: Mon.
Villa Josephine ★★★
French and Moroccan
cuisine on a terrace
overlooking the sea.
231 rue de la Montagne.
Tel: (039) 33 45 35; www.
villajosephine-tanger.com

Tetouan
Kabila Restaurant ★★
Hotel Kabila restaurant
offering fish and
European specialities.
Kabila Complex, 10km
(6 miles) north of Tetouan
at M'Diq on the route de
Sebta (P28 road). Tel:
(039) 97 50 13.

CENTRAL PLAINS,
MOYEN ATLAS AND
THE ATLANTIC COAST
Azrou
Hotel Panorama ★★
Fine French dining in an
Alpinesque location.
Azrou. Tel: (035) 56 20 10.

Casablanca
Taverne du Dauphin ★★
Good fish restaurant.
115 bd Houphoet Boigny.

Tel: (022) 22 12 00.
Closed: Sun.
Al Mounia ★★★
Set in a small garden by
an ancient dragon tree,
with excellent
Moroccan specialities.
95 rue Prince Moulay
Abdallah. Tel: (022) 22 26
69. Closed: Sun.
A Ma Bretagne ★★★★
This is Morocco's most
famous French restaurant,
serving a dazzling array of
fish and seafood. The high
standard of the kitchens
is matched by the price
of the food.
Aïn-Diab, boulevard Sidi
Abderrahmane.
Tel: (022) 36 21 12;
fax: (022) 94 41 55;
www.amabretagne.com
Closed: Sun & Aug.

Fès
Restaurant Laanibra ★
Moroccan dining in a
small medina palace.
61 Aïn Lkhail.
Tel: (035) 74 10 09.
Café Clock ★★
Delicious Moroccan and
international cuisine in
Fès' first expat-run
medina eaterie.
7 Derb el Magana, Talaa
Kebira. Tel: (035) 63 78
55; www.cafeclock.com

Al Fassia ★★★★
World-renowned Fès cuisine in elegant surroundings. Nightly floorshow.
Sofitel Palais Jamaï, Bab Guissa. Tel: (035) 63 43 31. Open for dinner.

Rabat
Le Petit Beur ★★★
A very popular Moroccan restaurant.
8 rue Damas.
Tel: (037) 73 13 22.
Villa Mandarine ★★★★
Sophisticated French dining in villa surrounds.
19 rue Ouled Bousbaa, Souissi. Tel: (037) 75 20 77; www.villamandarine.com

MARRAKECH AND HAUT ATLAS
Essaouira
Fish Stalls ★
Fresh fish grilled on barbecues by the harbour.
Chez Sam ★★★
A seafood institution perched on the edge of the docks.
Port de Pêche.
Tel: (024) 47 62 38.

Marrakech
Jemaa el Fna ★
Nothing compares to the taste of a grilled meal eaten on a wood bench in the heart of the chaotic Jemaa (*see pp88–9*).
Le Jacaranda ★★
Fine French cooking using local specialities.
32 boulevard Zerktouni, Guéliz.
Tel: (024) 44 72 15; www.lejacaranda.ma.
Open for lunch and dinner.
Restaurant El Fassia ★★
Run by a women's co-operative. Fez cuisine.
232 avenue Mohammed V. Tel: (024) 43 40 60.
Dar Moha ★★★
Some of Marrakech's best Moroccan-based food.
81 rue Dar el Bacha, Medina.
Tel: (024) 38 64 00; www darmoha.ma
L'Imperiale ★★★★
The showcase of the Hotel La Mamounia – evening dress required for a banquet at the height of luxury.
Hotel La Mamounia, avenue Bab Jdid.
Tel: (024) 38 86 00; www.mamounia.com.
Open: daily 8–11pm.
Restaurant Yacout ★★★★
Restored medina palace, on various floors.
79 Sidi Ahmed Soussi, east of Jemaa el Fna.
Tel: (024) 38 29 29.
Closed: Mon.

THE SOUTH
Agadir
La Miramar ★★
Italian restaurant specialising in seafood.
Boulevard Mohammed V. Tel: (088) 84 07 70.
La Pergola ★★
Rustic French restaurant.
Inezgane, km8 (5 miles) route d'Agadir.
Tel: (088) 27 18 01.

Ouarzazate
Chez Dimitri ★★
Opened in 1928 to serve the French Foreign Legion, Dimitri's is an Ouarzazate institution, offering French and Italian fare.
22 avenue Mohammed V. Tel: (024) 88 73 46.

Taroudannt
Taroudannt Hotel ★
Good French and Moroccan cuisine.
Place Assarag.
Tel: (028) 85 24 16.

CAFÉS
Casablanca
Patisserie Bennis
Delicious pastries.
Quartier Habous.
Tel: (022) 30 30 25.

Essaouira
Pâtisserie Driss
Orange juice, coffee and fresh croissants.
10 rue Hajali.
Tel: (024) 47 27 93.

Marrakech
Café Glacier and Café de la Place
Both overlook the Jemaa el Fna. The Café de France, also here, is more crowded and has less of a view.
East side of the Jemaa el Fna.
Dar Cherifa
The most chic café in town.
8 Derb Chorfa Lakbir.
Oliveri
A great place for ice creams and milkshakes.
9 boulevard el-Mansour Eddahbi.
Tel: (024) 44 89 13.

Rabat
Café Maure
Through the Andalusian garden of the kasbah, overlooking the estuary. Some delicious pastries.
Kasbah des Oudaïas.

Tanger
Café Central
The place of a thousand illicit deals. Unmissable.
Petit Socco.
Café Hafa
A favourite of writer Paul Bowles, with winning views.
La Masshan quarter.
Tel: (039) 93 84 44.

Café Tingis
A good place for people-watching.
Petit Socco.
Gran Café de Paris
A legacy of the colonial occupation.
Place de France.

Food and drink

Kebabs sizzling in the Jemaa el Fna, Marrakech

Moroccan food

Moroccan cuisine is renowned worldwide for its simple yet delicious recipes: succulent meat dishes, rich pastries and exotic fruits. Famed master-chef Robert Carrier even compiled his own book of Moroccan favourites. To experience the delights of a cuisine that is rivalled only by Turkey in the Muslim world, it is necessary to go beyond the precincts of the big hotels and seek out local traditional restaurants.

A traditional meal might start with *harira*, a thick spiced soup of vegetables and meat, commonly eaten to break the fast each sunset during Ramadan. Your waiter will whisper *'Bismillah'* – 'In the name of God' – as a sign for you to begin.

Next would come *mechoui*, the most impressive of Moroccan dishes – a whole lamb, roasted in a clay oven. In most restaurants *mechoui* must be ordered in advance. You tear off pieces of tender meat (always with your right hand only – the left is reserved for more basic functions) and eat them with round *khobza* bread.

If you are truly honoured, *pastilla* might follow, a delicate pastry stuffed with pigeon meat and almonds, coated with icing sugar. This is the great speciality of Fès and should not be missed.

Tajine, a national dish

Spices are important in Moroccan cuisine

The main course will be either *tajine* or *couscous*, Morocco's national dishes. *Tajine* is a meat or fish stew, delicately flavoured with olives. *Couscous* is served as the traditional Friday meal in the home: mountains of semolina served with stewed vegetables and mutton. In the south, *couscous* is cooked with onions and raisins, meat and vegetables being rare commodities. Traditionally *couscous* is eaten with the right hand, rolling the grains into a ball and dipping them into the sauce.

To finish this gastronomic feast, *cornes de gazelles* pastries are the most famous dessert – small crescents stuffed with almonds and honey.

These are washed down with *thé à la menthe* (mint tea).

Harira – thick spiced soup eaten at Ramadan

Hotels and accommodation

Morocco has always greeted visitors with warm hospitality, from the spice and gold traders of past centuries to the holidaymaker and business traveller of today. Cities like Casablanca, Fès and Marrakech contain numerous high-quality luxury hotels and riads *– indeed, the Mamounia in Marrakech is often cited as one of the top hotels in the world.*

Most Moroccan towns offer two distinct hotel districts: the medina and the New Town (Ville Nouvelle). Medina hotels, while close to the action and immersed in local life, may offer reduced security. However, the best *riads* (traditional Moroccan house) around the country are found in the medina. Some visitors stay in the new town, where the hotels are classified.

The north of Morocco is busiest in summer, and reservations are recommended. Mountain resorts are also busy, particularly in the Middle Atlas. Further south, high season tends to be from October to April, especially around Marrakech and down to Ouarzazate. Christmas and Easter are busy throughout Morocco and it is advisable to book in advance.

Standards of service and hygiene are generally good, although in small towns and villages facilities are naturally more limited. Many down-market hotels

The Beach Club Hotel at Agadir

have private bathroom facilities in each room, although it is rare to find a plug, due to the Muslim tradition of washing under running water. There have been recent water shortages in some parts of Morocco – use water conscientiously.

Categories and prices

Each classification has A and B ratings, which can vary slightly in amenities and price.

5-star: more than 2,300DH (dirhams) per night

4-star A+B: 350DH–700DH

3-star A+B: 250DH–400DH

2-star A+B: 150DH–300DH

1-star A+B: 70DH–200DH

Travellers who purchase their travel tickets from a Thomas Cook network location are entitled to use the services of any other Thomas Cook network location, free of charge, to make hotel reservations.

Dos and don'ts

Room prices should include a 20 per cent tax, and be posted at hotel reception. Prices indicated are maximum prices for the hotel in the particular category. Off-season it may be possible to get special rates. For four- and five-star hotels it is advisable to book in advance, as these establishments rely on tour groups and may be reluctant to accept individual travellers on the spot. The ONMT tourist office in each town will be able to help with hotel reservations.

It is unwise to drink tap water (most upmarket hotels supply mineral water), and therefore ice cubes should be avoided too. Many modern hotels now rely on solar power for hot water heating, and consequently supplies of hot water in the evening are not infinite. Tipping is only expected in five-star hotels – 10DH is sufficient.

Where to stay

To get the most out of your holiday try to mix your accommodation, spending some nights in cheaper places and

HOTELS PALAIS

If you have ever dreamt of sleeping in a palace, Morocco is the place to do it. A handful of opulent palaces have been converted into some of the world's most luxurious hotels, the Hotels Palais. Of these the most famous is the **Sofitel Palais Jamaï** in Fès, the 19th-century residence of the Jamaï family, viziers to Sultan Moulay Hassan. The hotel boasts some magnificent suites with views over the medina. The new block enjoys incredible views. Morocco's top hotel, one of the top hotels in the world, is the **Mamounia** in Marrakech. Once an Alaouite palace, the newly refurbished Mamounia was a favourite of Winston Churchill and offers the last word in luxury. Further south, near Taroudannt, **La Gazelle d'Or** was once home to a French baron, with views up to the High Atlas – its grass is still cut by hand. In Taroudannt itself, **Hotel Palais Salam** is an 18th-century palace built into the town's medieval walls. In keeping with this luxurious tradition, two more hotels have been built according to the lavish standards of the Hotels Palais – the **Jnan Palace** in Fès, and the **Palmeraie Golf Palace** in Marrakech, both of which offer sumptuous surroundings and excellent service.

Breakfast in splendour at Le Royal Mansour
Méridien in Casablanca

Mansour Méridien in Casablanca offer all mod-cons – fine restaurants, discos, cocktail bars, 24-hour room service and business facilities. Prices compare favourably with equivalent accommodation in Europe and North America. Four-star hotels are plentiful and offer high standards of service and cleanliness without the luxury of five-star accommodation.

Riad accommodation

Many people now travel to Morocco to experience the magic of staying in a converted traditional home. Expect chic luxury, gorgeous décor and charm. This experience is not to be missed.

Standard accommodation

Mid-range accommodation varies considerably, but still maintains good standards at inexpensive prices. Many three-star hotels offer swimming pools. Much standard accommodation dates from the French occupation, and retains a certain venerable charm. **Hotel Balima**, in Rabat, with huge rooms and fading red upholstery, was the first purpose-built hotel in Morocco, completed in 1932.

splashing out on top-class hotels or luxury *riads* when the occasion arises. Morocco is one of the few countries where you can alternate between the two ends of the hotel market and still enjoy a warm welcome and authentic accommodation.

Four- and five-star accommodation

Morocco's top-quality accommodation rivals any in the world. Hotels like the **Jnan Palace** in Fès or **Le Royal**

Budget accommodation

Morocco has no lack of budget accommodation, such as guesthouses (*riads*) and hostels (although they are probably called hotels). Most are found in the medinas of Moroccan towns. Here, you are close to the action and able to participate in everyday

Moroccan life; conversely, you are in a confusing maze of streets, often faced with lower-standard rooms and plumbing, and cannot guarantee the security of your belongings. At best, medina hotels are cheap, immaculate, with whitewashed rooms around a central airy courtyard. Such paradise is more likely to be found in smaller towns: **Casa Hassan** in the middle of Chefchaouen's medina and **Hotel des Remparts** in Essaouira are good examples of medina accommodation at its best. Outside the medina,

FAMILY HOTELS

Another relic of French occupation in Morocco is the scattering of small family-run hotels, similar to French country auberges. Usually found in rural areas, especially the Middle and High Atlas, they are inexpensive, sometimes rudimentary but always welcoming. Many are preserved much as they were during the French Protectorate, with red-checked tablecloths, fine wine cellars and stuffed animals over the bar. Of these the most enchanting are **Gite de Charme**, south of Azrou in the Middle Atlas, and **Au Sanglier qui Fume**, at Ouirgane. A more modern approach is found at **Villa Maroc**, in Essaouira, a renovated former brothel run by an English couple.

one- and two-star hotels are more secure and more likely to enjoy running water.

Most Moroccan cities have campsites, but generally they do not yet meet Western standards.

Young families

Along the Mediterranean and Atlantic coasts, some of the best-value accommodation is to be found in tourist villages. These complexes offer small apartment accommodation around central shared facilities such as swimming pools, tennis courts, playgrounds and restaurants and are ideal for young families. On the Mediterranean coast, resorts such as **Kabila**, **Cabo Negro** and the newly built **MarinaSmir** are havens for those with young children – safe, attractively designed, close to the sea and inexpensive. On the Atlantic coast, Agadir has no fewer than 30 such 'villages' to suit all tastes and pockets.

The sun-filled rooftops of the Villa Maroc in Essaouira

On business

Banking has been restructured, but remains highly regulated. Moroccan banks operate under one of the toughest lending limits in the world at 7 per cent of net capital funds per borrower. When setting up a company in Morocco it is necessary to open a Moroccan bank account, where at least a quarter of the capital investment should be deposited.

Business hours

Most times in Morocco are counted using the 24-hour clock. Hours may vary in summer and during Ramadan.

Banks

Monday to Friday, 8.30–11.30am and 2.30–3.30pm.

Business offices

Monday to Friday 9am–1pm and 3–6pm.

Government offices

Monday to Friday 8.30am–noon and 2.30–6pm.

Capital investment

Foreigners may invest foreign capital in Morocco as hard currency, tangible fixed assets (eg machinery, tools) or intangible fixed assets (eg patents, trademarks). Transfer of the capital invested, any income generated by that capital and any capital gains realised is permitted.

Chambers of commerce

Federation of Moroccan Chambers of Commerce, *6 rue Erfoud, PO Box 218,*

Rabat. Tel: (037) 76 70 51; fax: (037) 76 70 76.

British Chamber of Commerce for Morocco, *65 avenue Hassan Seghir, Casablanca. Tel: (022) 44 88 60; fax: (022) 44 88 68; www.bccm.co.ma*

Conference facilities

Casablanca

The largest conference facilities are provided by **Le Royal Mansour Méridien**, *27 avenue des FAR. Tel: (022) 31 30 11; www.starwoodhotels.com*

Fès

The **Jnan Palace** offers a 1,300-person capacity. *Avenue Ahmed Chaouki. Tel: (035) 65 39 65; fax: (035) 65 19 17; www.sogatour.ma*

Marrakech

The vast **Palmeraie Golf Palace** combines a 1,200-person conference capacity with an 18-hole golf course. *Les Jardins de la Palmeraie. Tel: (024) 36 87 04; fax: (024) 30 20 20; www.pgpmarrakech.com.* Also in Marrakech, the **Palais des Congrès de**

Marrakech can provide 16 fully equipped conference rooms with 25- to 2,800-person capacity.

Etiquette
Remember that Morocco is a Muslim state. It is best not to schedule business meetings for Friday, the day of prayer.

Exchange rate
In January 1993 the Moroccan dirham was made convertible for all transactions on current account by foreign investors and Moroccan residents abroad. This makes it easier to transfer funds in and out of the country. Otherwise the Moroccan dirham is not freely convertible, and cannot be exchanged outside Morocco.

Exhibition organisers
Casablanca
Archoun Tourisme, *9 Gihali Ahmed. Tel: (022) 27 11 30; fax: (022) 27 55 00.*
Atlas Voyages, *44 avenue des FAR. Tel: (022) 46 01 00; fax: (022) 31 69 02; www.atlasvoyages.com*
KTI, *3 rue des Hirondelles, Rond Point Racine. Tel: (022) 39 85 72; fax: (022) 39 85 67; www.ktivoyages.com*

Government agencies
Two important government agencies promoting business growth in Morocco are the **Office for Industrial Development**, *10 Zenkat Gandhi, Rabat (tel: (037) 70 84 60; fax: (037) 70 76 95)*, and the **Centre Marocain de Promotion des Exportations**,

23 boulevard Girardot, Casablanca (tel: (022) 30 22 10; fax: (022) 30 17 93; www.cpmpe.org.ma).

Internet access *See p182.*

Language
The main language of business is still French, with English a close second.

Media
L'Economiste provides balanced and reliable market information.

Premises
Any company wishing to be recognised by the Moroccan authorities must have an office in Morocco. Foreigners may buy property only with foreign currency.

Tax
Those who may be eligible for taxation should seek advice.

Foreign individuals and diplomats are exempt from income tax. Foreigners who live in Morocco for more than six consecutive months must pay tax.

Translation services
International Congress Star, *15 rue al Madina, Hassan, Rabat. Tel: (037) 20 41 39; fax: (037) 70 74 75; www.congressstartranslations.com*

Work permits
These are required by foreigners wishing to work in Morocco.

Mint tea

The Moroccan tea ceremony is a complex custom but a simple pleasure

Mint tea is the lifeblood of Morocco and you will be offered it wherever you go. More than mere refreshment, more than mere social lubrication, a glass of mint tea is an avowal of friendship, and should not be rejected at any time. It is drunk day and night, often in vast quantities. Green Chinese tea is used, originally introduced by British traders in the 1800s. The mint is Moroccan, the best variety coming from Meknès. The tea is always very sweet, with plenty of sugar.

Apart from its culinary role as a refreshing summer drink and a warming winter tipple, mint tea is also highly symbolic. The green of the tea is also the green of the Prophet Muhammad, and thus brings great good luck. Green is also the colour of fertility, the most prestigious of Moroccan blessings. The high sugar content is a token of sweet friendship and a blessing for continuous good health.

Attending a tea ceremony is one of the classic pleasures of visiting Morocco. The ceremony is ancient and learnt from an early age. An honoured guest is chosen to make the tea, and sits cross-legged while a tray is set before him (honoured guests are usually male). On the tray are a silver teapot, small glasses and three boxes of tea, mint and sugar. In awed silence, a pinch of tea is put in the teapot and boiling water added, followed by sugar and fresh mint. The teapot is then left to infuse. The guest eventually pours a taste for himself, which he swirls dramatically around his mouth; if satisfied, he pours for the others, always from a great height to ensure the tea is well mixed and that his presentation is amply appreciated. Guests must then drink at least three glasses for the host to be sure they have accepted his hospitality.

Practical guide

Arriving

Travellers from the UK or Ireland, New Zealand, Australia, Canada and the USA do not require a visa for stays of 90 days or less. South African nationals require a visa. All categories of traveller must be in possession of a valid passport. Travellers who require visas should obtain them in their country of residence.

By air

Numerous international airlines fly to Morocco's main Mohammed V Airport outside Casablanca. The most regular flights are available from Royal Air Maroc (RAM), the state airline, which also provides connections to all other Moroccan cities. Direct flights from London Heathrow and Gatwick airports to Moroccan destinations are increasing all the time and currently at the time of writing there are direct flights to Agadir, Casablanca, Fès, Marrakech and Tanger. Some of these are currently seasonal. The most frequent flights are to Casablanca and Marrakech.
Royal Air Maroc, *32–3 Garfield St, London (tel: (020) 7307 5800; www.royalairmaroc.com)*, easyJet (*www.easyjet.com*), Ryanair (*www.ryanair.com*), Atlas Blue (*www.atlas-blue.com*) and Thomsonfly (*www.thomsonfly.com*) currently operate direct flights from the UK to Morocco. *Flythomascook.com* have flights from a number of British airports to Agadir.

For details of flight arrivals and departures when in Morocco contact National Airports Authority (ONDA), *Mohammed V Airport, Casablanca (tel: (081) 00 02 24; www.onda.org.ma)*.

From Mohammed V Airport a train leaves every hour for the 30-minute journey to Casablanca Voyageurs station. If you are going to Rabat you need to stay on the train to the last stop at Ain Sebaa station. From here there is a train every 30 minutes to Rabat. Regular buses run by CTM leave the airport for the centre of Casablanca. Taxis are also available from outside the airport. The time it takes to get into the centre of Casablanca depends on the notorious traffic.

By car

The most frequent ferries are from Algeciras in Spain to Tanger or Ceuta. In the summer there are many daily crossings of the Strait and it is one of the most economical ways to enter Morocco. Ferries operate less frequently in the winter and crossing times are of course dependent on the weather.

By rail

Sleepers depart daily from Paris to Madrid (13 hours), where passengers must change trains for Algeciras (11 hours). The *Thomas Cook Overseas Timetable* gives details of many rail, bus and shipping services worldwide, and will help you plan a rail journey to, from and around Morocco. It is available in the UK from some stations, any branch of Thomas Cook, or by phoning *(01733) 416477* or online at *www.thomascookpublishing.com*. Also consult *www.oncf.ma*

Camping

Camping is widespread in Morocco and most major cities have campsites located in the outskirts. Campsites are generally not of European standard but vary in quality depending on where you are in the country. Some have good showering and toilet facilities; others have very little, if any, and may even only be patches of level ground. It can cost as little as 15DH for a site, so it is quite an economical way to see the country. 'Camping' in Arabic is '*moukhayyem*'.

Climate

The northern half of the country has two distinct seasons: winter is wet and mild along the coast and icy in the mountains, with temperatures below freezing. Summer is hot and sunny.

In the south it is either hot or hotter with temperatures rising to 45°C (113°F). Nights can get cool in winter.

WEATHER CONVERSION CHART

25.4mm = 1 inch
°F = 1.8 × °C + 32

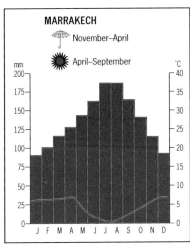

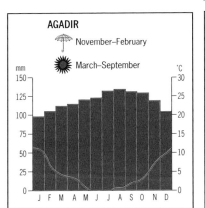

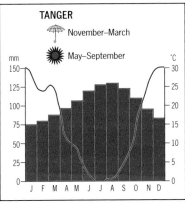

Crime

Violent crime rates are very low. Petty thefts are, however, commonplace – take sensible precautions, especially in cities. Carry only small amounts of cash and use a money belt for passports and valuables.

When driving, do not leave luggage and valuables accessible in the car. Most horror stories involve drug transactions – the police are less than sympathetic for a tourist threatened over a drug deal.

Customs regulations

On entry, duty-free limits are 200 cigarettes, 1 litre of spirits, 25cl of perfume. The import of all narcotics is forbidden and carries stiff prison sentences. There is no restriction on the import of foreign currency but the Moroccan dirham cannot be imported or exported.

Driving

Car hire

Car hire is expensive in Morocco. The cheapest deals for car hire are usually available on the internet. All the main international companies have representatives in Morocco:
Avis (*www.avis.com*),
Budget (*www.budget.com*),
Europcar (*www.europcar.com*) and
Hertz (*www.hertz.com*) all have offices in Moroccan cities. Local hire companies sometimes offer cheaper deals, but there is no guarantee of the quality of service.

To drive a car in Morocco you must be over 21 and possess a full driver's licence. It is a good idea to have your passport with you, especially if your driver's licence doesn't have a photo identity. Always check that the spare tyre is in good condition, and try the brakes if possible. The only legally required insurance is third party, but it is advisable to take out the extra collision damage waiver and personal accident insurance to cover all possible eventualities.

Emergencies

In an emergency contact the nearest police post. You will find police road checks every 70km (45 miles) or so – these are standard throughout Morocco, and you will be asked for your driving papers.

Insurance

If you are bringing a car from Europe make sure your insurance includes a Green Card that covers Morocco. If it does not you will be able to buy insurance on arriving at frontier posts; apart from Green Cards, insurance policies are not valid unless they have been issued by a company with an office in Morocco.

The Moroccan Insurance Bureau is **Bureau Central Marocain d'Assurances**,
154 boulevard d'Anfa 101, Casablanca (tel: (022) 39 18 57;
fax: (022) 39 39 34;
email: bcma-sec@casanet.ma).

Parking

Everywhere you stop, someone will appear offering to 'guard' your vehicle. These attendants are the Moroccan equivalent of the parking meter and a vital part of the local economy; 2DH is a usual fee for daytime parking, 5DH for overnight.

Petrol

Petrol and diesel are widely available. Unleaded (*sans plomb*) is still not the norm but is becoming more common. It is still difficult to get in remote areas so fill up before you leave urban areas. In remote locations, especially in the south, fill up the tank whenever possible so you avoid running the risk of being stranded.

The sand dunes of Diabat

Roads

Morocco has a major plan to update its road system and many new motorways are being built. The national motorway (*autoroute nationale*), given an N notation, runs between most major cities and includes some toll roads. Smaller roads have P and R notations.

In winter some mountain passes may be blocked by snow. In spring beware of flash floods in river valleys, especially in the High Atlas and the south. Further information is available from the **Touring Club of Morocco**, *3 avenue des FAR, Casablanca (tel: (022) 26 52 31)*.

Speed limits

Limits are 100kmh (62mph) outside towns, and 40kmh (25mph) within town limits.

Drugs

Historically, most of the marijuana exported to Europe originated in Morocco. However, in recent years the authorities have been cracking down on the cultivation and trafficking of the drug and those caught in possession face prison sentences. Do not, in any circumstances, accept packages from strangers, and avoid the kif-growing areas of the Rif.

Electricity

Most installations are 220V, but in small towns 110V may be in use. Sockets take European-style two-pin plugs.

Embassies and consulates

Australia: c/o Canada
Canada: Rabat Embassy,
13 Jaffar as-Sadik, Agdal, Rabat
(tel: (037) 68 74 00; www.rabat.gc.ca).
New Zealand: c/o UK
Republic of Ireland: c/o UK
UK: Casablanca Consulate General,
Villa les Salurges, 36 rue de la Loire, Polo
(tel: (022) 85 74 00; fax: (022) 83 46 25).
Rabat Embassy,
28 avenue SAR Sidi Mohammed, Souissi
(tel: (037) 63 33 33; fax: (037) 75 87 09;
email: british@mtds.com;
www.britain.org.ma).
Tanger Consulate,
9 rue d'Amerique du Sud
(tel: (039) 93 69 39).
USA: Casablanca Consulate,
8 boulevard Moulay Youssef (tel: (022)
20 41 27).
Rabat Embassy,
2 avenue de Mohammed el Fassi (tel:
(037) 76 22 65; fax: (037) 76 56 61;
www.usembassy.ma).

Emergency telephone numbers

Police *19*
Fire service/Ambulance *15*

Health and insurance

Up-to-date health advice can be
obtained from your Thomas Cook
travel consultant. There are no
mandatory vaccination requirements,
and no vaccination recommendations
other than to keep tetanus and polio
immunisation up to date. Like every
other part of the world, HIV is present.

Medical insurance is advisable, as part
of a travel insurance package.

Strict food and water hygiene is
essential to avoid problems with
diarrhoea. Make sure food has been
properly prepared; drink boiled or
bottled water only, and remember that
ice cubes will have been made with tap
water. In the south, do not bathe in
rivers, as bilharzia is prevalent.

Pharmacies are widespread and
well stocked with European medicines.
Most pharmacists speak French, but
local tourist offices will be able to
direct you to an English-speaking
chemist.

Hitchhiking

Hitchhiking is possible in rural areas
but is not recommended. In areas
where bus services are infrequent, locals
will pay the equivalent of a bus ticket
for a ride in a private vehicle – you will
be expected to do the same. Never
hitchhike alone.

Internet access

Most major hotels and *riads* will be able
to offer access to the internet. Internet
cafés are springing up all over the
country and you should easily find one
in any of the major cities or resorts. Ask
at your hotel.

Maps

The most widely available and inclusive
road map of Morocco is the red
Michelin number 969. More detailed
maps of hiking are available in many

LANGUAGE

Morocco's first language is Arabic, although up to 40 per cent of the population speaks Berber dialects. French is widely spoken, and many Moroccans are bilingual Arabic-French.

ARABIC

While it is impossible to learn Moroccan Arabic over a short stay, employing a few key phrases will impress and amuse your hosts, and may aid the bargaining process in souks. Most Moroccans speak some French. The Arabic Language Institute in Fès runs regular language courses:
PO Box 2136, Fès.
Tel: (035) 62 48 50; fax: (035) 93 16 08;
www.alif-fes.com

PRONUNCIATION

There are no silent letters – pronounce all that is written.
kh = ch (like Scottish loch) as in
Msa l'khir = Msa l'chir
gh = like the French rolling 'r' as in
gheda = rreda
ai = like 'eye' as in baggai = bageye
q = like k as in qreeb = kreeb
j = like s in 'sure' as in joob = soob

NUMBERS

Arabic numbers are based on symbols 1–9.

1 *wahèd*	**10** *achra*
2 *jooj*	**20** *chrin*
3 *tlàta*	**50** *khamsin*
4 *àrba*	**1,000** *alef*
5 *khàmsa*	
6 *sètta*	
7 *sèba*	
8 *tmènia*	
9 *tseud*	

Everyday expressions

Hello (informal)	*la bes*
Hello (more formal)	*salamalaykoom*
Goodbye	*beslamah*
Good morning	*sbah el khir*
Good afternoon	*msa el khir*
Good night	*leela saieeda*
Please	*minfadlik*
Thank you	*choukrane*
Yes/no	*wakha/la*
Where is?	*fayn kayn?*
How much?	*bsh hal?*
Too expensive	*ghalee bzef*
Cheaper	*rkhiss*
Okay	*wakha*
Big	*kebir*
Small	*seghir*
Go away	*emshee*
Today	*elyoum*
Yesterday	*elbarah*
Tomorrow	*ghedda*

Days of the week

Sunday	*nhar el had*
Monday	*nhar el tnin*
Tuesday	*nahr el tlata*
Wednesday	*nhar el arba*
Thursday	*nhar el khemis*
Friday	*el jmaa*
Saturday	*nhat es sebt*

bookshops, and at Imlil, departure point for the Mount Toubkal ascent.

Measurements and sizes
See p185.

Media
British and French newspapers are available in big cities. The *International Herald Tribune* is also easy to find. Local press is divided between French and Arabic dailies. The main French papers are the pro-government *Le Matin du Sahara*, the opposition *L'Opinion* and the communist *Al-Bayanne*. Of the Arabic papers, *Al-Alam*, loyal to the Istiqlal party, has the widest circulation.

BBC World Service is theoretically found on short wave 15.07MHz and 17.705MHz. Most large hotels have satellite TV, receiving CNN News and European Sky News. Moroccan television broadcasts many programmes in French.

Money matters
The Moroccan dirham (DH) is not exchangeable outside Morocco. It is illegal to import or export Moroccan dirhams. When nearing the end of your stay it is wise to shed as many of your dirhams as possible, budgeting carefully. To exchange dirhams on leaving Morocco you must show your exchange receipts – you can change back 50 per cent of the sums totalled on your receipts.

Most small towns have banks at which you can change traveller's cheques. The rate is fixed by the government and there is little competition between banks. Big hotels also change traveller's cheques at rates similar to, if not better than, banks. Credit cards are taken in most large hotels and up-market restaurants; Visa is the most widely accepted.

US dollar, sterling, euro and Swiss franc traveller's cheques are all accepted. Major hotels and some restaurants and shops in main tourist and commercial areas accept traveller's cheques in lieu of cash.

National holidays
Official holidays
1 January New Year's Day
11 January Manifesto of Independence
1 May Labour Day
30 July Feast of the Throne
14 August Allegiance of Oued Ed-Dahab
21 August Youth Day (King's Birthday)
6 November Green March Anniversary
18 November Independence Day

Opening hours
Hours may vary in summer and during Ramadan.
Banks
Monday to Friday 8.30–11.30am and 2–3.30pm.
Government offices
Monday to Friday 8.30am–noon and 2.30–6pm.
Museums
Weekly 8.30am–noon and 3–6pm. Sometimes closed on Tuesdays.
Shops
Weekly 9am–7pm (in practice most close for lunch).

Photography

Film is widely available, at comparable prices to European countries. For photographs in towns, especially in medinas, where there is contrast between light and shade, fast film is useful – 400 ASA. Slower film is better for landscape shots. If you've gone digital, be sure to take your charger and a large memory card.

Always ask before taking someone's picture, and never insist. Street entertainers expect payment for a picture (they are, after all, putting on a professional show). Do not give money to children to take their pictures – they will prefer modelling to schooling.

Places of worship

St Andrew's English Church in Tanger is the only Anglican church in Morocco and has weekly services. Otherwise there are numerous Catholic churches, even in many of the smaller towns. The main synagogue is in Casablanca, with others in Tanger and Marrakech. Islamic beliefs are understandably well catered for.

Police

There are two types of police in Morocco – the *gendarmerie*, dressed in khaki with green berets, and the *sûreté nationale*, who wear grey. The *gendarmerie* deal more with internal security, while the *sûreté nationale* carry out local policing in towns and are responsible for tourists.

CONVERSION TABLE

FROM	TO	MULTIPLY BY
Inches	Centimetres	2.54
Feet	Metres	0.3048
Yards	Metres	0.9144
Miles	Kilometres	1.6090
Acres	Hectares	0.4047
Gallons	Litres	4.5460
Ounces	Grams	28.35
Pounds	Grams	453.6
Pounds	Kilograms	0.4536
Tons	Tonnes	1.0160

To convert back, for example from centimetres to inches, divide by the number in the third column.

MEN'S SUITS

UK	36	38	40	42	44	46	48
Rest of Europe	46	48	50	52	54	56	58
USA	36	38	40	42	44	46	48

DRESS SIZES

UK	8	10	12	14	16	18
France	36	38	40	42	44	46
Italy	38	40	42	44	46	48
Rest of Europe	34	36	38	40	42	44
USA	6	8	10	12	14	16

MEN'S SHIRTS

UK	14	14.5	15	15.5	16	16.5	17
Rest of Europe	36	37	38	39/40	41	42	43
USA	14	14.5	15	15.5	16	16.5	17

MEN'S SHOES

UK	7	7.5	8.5	9.5	10.5	11
Rest of Europe	41	42	43	44	45	46
USA	8	8.5	9.5	10.5	11.5	12

WOMEN'S SHOES

UK	4.5	5	5.5	6	6.5	7
Rest of Europe	38	38	39	39	40	41
USA	6	6.5	7	7.5	8	8.5

The police emergency telephone number is *19*.

Post offices

Moroccan post offices demand perseverance and resilience. With 2 million Moroccans working abroad, postal communications are stretched to their limits – queues are part of the experience. Letters take about a week to get to Europe, two to North America and Australasia. Stamps are more rapidly purchased in tourist shops and hotels. Post offices are open Monday to Friday 8.30am–noon and 3–6pm in winter and 8am–3pm in summer.

Public transport
Air
Royal Air Maroc (RAM) (*www.royalairmaroc.com*) serves most major towns within Morocco and has offices throughout the country. Flying is relatively inexpensive and is highly recommended to cover long distances (Tanger–Marrakech and particularly to

the deep south and La'youne). RAM has ticket reservation offices in all major cities in the country. The main offices of RAM are: Agadir, *avenue Général Kettani (tel: (028) 82 91 20)*, Casablanca, *44 avenue des FAR (tel: (022) 46 41 00)*, Marrakech, *197 avenue Mohammed V (tel: (024) 42 55 01)* and Tanger, *place de France (tel: (039) 93 47 22)*.

Regional Airlines (RAL), *Mohammed V Airport, Casablanca (tel: (022) 53 69 40)*, its local competitor, is more expensive and more suited for business travel (*www.regionalmaroc.com*).

Buses
Bus services between towns are often full and it is necessary to reserve in advance. The main company is the national carrier CTM (*www.ctm.co.ma*). Costs are marginally cheaper than *grands taxis*, but journeys take much longer. There are numerous small private outfits, all of which will approach you at bus stations:

RELIGIOUS HOLIDAYS

The main religious festival is that of Ramadan (*see p26*). The dates for religious festivals follow the lunar calendar and therefore move backwards by 11 days each year. Approximate dates are as follows:

	2009	2010	2011
Start of Ramadan	22 Aug	11 Aug	1 Aug
Aid el-Fitr	21 Sept	10 Sept	30 Aug
Aid al-Adha (**Festival of Sacrifice**)	28 Nov	17 Nov	6 Nov
Muslim New Year (**Muharram**)	29 Dec	7 Dec	20 Nov
Prophet's Birthday	9 Mar	26 Feb	15 Feb

these are far from reliable and it is best to stick to the main carriers.

Taxis

Within towns *petits taxis* (small taxis, often Fiats) are cheap and efficient. By law fares should be determined by a meter – insist on the *compteur* being turned on. A battle of will might ensue, but always remember the law is on your side. After 10pm the driver can add 50 per cent to the metered fare.

Routes between towns are served by *grands taxis*: usually large, antiquated Mercedes. These depart from designated taxi stations, and have the advantage of being quicker than buses and not bound to timetables. You pay a fixed rate per place in the car, which will leave only when it is full (usually six passengers). If you want to leave before the driver has found six passengers you must pay for the empty places.

Trains

Trains are efficient and fairly comfortable in Morocco, but offer a limited number of routes. For longer journeys it may be preferable to pay a little extra for a first-class seat, as these are more spacious and comfortable. Most stations are conveniently situated in the new quarters of Moroccan towns, close to hotels. Only a few have left-luggage offices – hotels and even cafés may lock up bags for a small fee. For further information, contact Office National des Chemins de Fer, ONCF,

Casablanca railway station

www.oncf.ma. The website is in French and Arabic only.

Student and youth travel

The International Student Card is largely redundant in Morocco – there are no student reductions on museum and site entry. RAM (*see opposite*) offers 25 per cent discount on internal flights to students when tickets are bought in advance, and ONCF offers 50 per cent discounts on a package of more than eight return train trips within Morocco. European Interail passes extend to the Moroccan rail system.

Sustainable tourism

Thomas Cook is a strong advocate of ethical and fairly traded tourism and believes that the travel experience should be as good for the places visited as it is for the people who visit them. That's why we firmly support The Travel Foundation, a charity that develops solutions to help improve and protect holiday destinations, their environment, traditions and culture. To find out what you can do to make a positive difference to the places you travel to and the people who live there, please visit
www.thetravelfoundation.org.uk

Telephones and faxes

Mobile phone coverage (061 to 068 numbers) is about 90 per cent in Morocco and two major local companies provide service, Maroc Telecom and Méditel. The network runs on the European 900MHz GSM standard and on the 1800MHz frequency. So your mobile will work if your provider has a roaming agreement with one of the two Moroccan providers. Roaming calls are expensive and you can rent out a local mobile phone for prolonged stays in the country or if you envisage making a lot of calls. Make sure there is no SIM lock active on your phone.

There are two ways to make a landline telephone call from Morocco. The first is at the post office, where you make a direct call in a designated telephone cubicle. Once the call is finished you pay for the units used at a central desk. There are now also phones that take telephone cards – these are found outside post offices. Cards are sold in post offices, in local shops and by legions of young men who hang around the phones.

The second possibility is to call from your hotel – much easier, but three times the cost of calling from the post office.

For local calls dial the area code then the number. For international calls dial *00* and the country code, then the area code (minus the *0*) followed by the number. The country code for the UK is *44*, Ireland is *353*, USA and Canada is *1*, Australia is *61* and New Zealand is *64*. Within Morocco important numbers are:

16 Directory enquiries
10 Operator
120 International operator

Main local codes were changed in 2006 and are as follows:
Agadir and region – *088*, Casablanca – *022*, El-Jadida – *023*, Fès and region – *035*, Marrakech and region – *024*, Mohammedia – *02*, Oujda and region – *036*, Rabat – *037*, Tanger and region – *039*.

Spanish enclaves of Ceuta and Melilla have their own international code. To dial a number in Morocco from these Spanish enclaves you have to first dial

00-212. For Ceuta and Melilla, there are nine-digit numbers without a prefix. You can call these numbers from Spain directly but need to use the prefix *0034* from Morocco. The first three digits of Ceuta and Melilla numbers are *952*.

Most of the larger hotels will offer internet access. All big hotels can fax for you, although charges are much higher than in Europe and North America. There are also shops which specialise in faxing, although these are often more expensive than hotels.

Time

Morocco follows GMT all year.

Tipping

You will be expected to tip in Morocco. Always carry small change to pay parking attendants, guides and waiters. Even if a service charge is included it is customary to pay an extra 7–10 per cent to the waiter. In big hotels valets expect 10DH for their services.

Islam encourages the giving of alms (*zakat*) and most Moroccans give generously to beggars in the street. An offering of a few coins (a paltry sum in Western terms) is a customary gesture.

Toilets

Moroccan toilets do not have the best reputation. Where tourists congregate they are comparable with Western toilets; elsewhere things are little more than rudimentary. It is wise to carry a roll of toilet paper. Courage is of the essence.

Tourist offices

Each Moroccan town has its tourist office, the ONMT. Several towns also possess Syndicats d'Initiatives, which provide similar facilities. The main tourist offices can be found in the following locations:

Agadir, *Immeuble Ignouan, avenue Mohammed V. Tel: (088) 84 63 77; fax: (088) 84 63 78.*

Casablanca, *55 rue Omar Slaoui. Tel: (022) 27 11 77; fax: (022) 20 59 29.*

Fès, *place Mohammed V. Tel: (035) 62 47 69.*

Marrakech, *place Abdelmoumen Ben Ali, Guéliz. Tel: (024) 43 61 31; fax: (024) 43 60 57.*

Meknès, *27 place Administrative. Tel: (035) 51 60 22.*

Ouarzazate, *avenue Mohammed V. Tel: (024) 88 24 85; fax: (024) 88 52 90.*

Rabat, *Rue Zellaha, Agdal. Tel: (037) 67 40 13; fax: (037) 67 40 15.*

Tanger, *29 boulevard Pasteur. Tel: (039) 94 86 69; fax: (039) 94 86 61.*

Tetouan, *30 avenue Mohammed V. Tel: (039) 96 19 16; fax: (039) 96 19 14.*

Travellers with disabilities

There are few specially adapted facilities for disabled travellers. Most moderate to expensive hotels have lift services and some, like the Jnan Palace in Fès, have wheelchair ramps. Wheelchairs are available at all international airports. The Moroccan National Tourist Office can provide information on your destination prior to departure. *www.visitmorocco.com*

Index

Acknowledgements

Thomas Cook wishes to thank the following photographers, libraries and other organisations for their assistance in the preparation of this book, and to whom the copyright belongs.

AA PHOTO LIBRARY/IAN BURGUM 10, 12, 13, 18, 26, 34, 35, 36, 40, 41, 43, 45, 47, 48, 54, 55, 59, 62, 67, 71, 72, 73, 76, 77, 79, 82, 83, 93, 94, 95, 98, 100, 102, 105, 106, 107, 108, 109, 110, 115, 117, 118, 122, 123, 125, 128, 129, 132, 137, 139, 143, 147, 150, 151, 156, 167, 169b, 170, 172, 173, 177a, 177b, 181
AA PHOTO LIBRARY/PAUL KENWARD 29, 30, 57, 60, 61, 66, 85, 91, 92, 120, 126, 127, 133, 136, 155, 176
BIG STOCK PHOTO 25 (Michael Ransburg), 33 (Kwieciszewski Warszawa), 49 (Craig Birkdale), 168 (Laurent Renault)
CLAIRE BOOBBYER 23, 68, 140
CONOR CAFFREY 11, 89, 159
FLICKR 15 (Ahron de Leeuw), 27 (Jon Cohen), 52 (Andy Wright), 134 (Rui Ornelas)
FOTOLIA 121 (Mohammed Mali)
FOTOSEARCH 21, 187 (Flat Earth)
PICTURES COLOUR LIBRARY 144, 148
TOURISME MAROCAIN 157
WIKIMEDIA COMMONS 70 (Fabos), 90 (Luc Viatour), 141, 169a (Bertrand Devouard)
WORLD PICTURES 1, 101

For CAMBRIDGE PUBLISHING MANAGEMENT LTD:
Project editor: Rosalind Munro
Typesetter: Trevor Double
Proofreader: Karolin Thomas

SEND YOUR THOUGHTS TO BOOKS@THOMASCOOK.COM

We're committed to providing the very best up-to-date information in our travel guides and constantly strive to make them as useful as they can be. You can help us to improve future editions by letting us have your feedback. If you've made a wonderful discovery on your travels that we don't already feature, if you'd like to inform us about recent changes to anything that we do include, or if you simply want to let us know your thoughts about this guidebook and how we can make it even better – we'd love to hear from you.

Send us ideas, discoveries and recommendations today and then look out for your valuable input in the next edition of this title.

Emails to the above address, or letters to Travellers Series Editor, Thomas Cook Publishing, PO Box 227, Coningsby Road, Peterborough PE3 8SB, UK.

Please don't forget to let us know which title your feedback refers to!